THE EVERYTHING KIDS'

Math Puzzles
for
Kindergarten

Learn about Counting, Measuring, Adding,
and More with 100 Fun Puzzles!

Hannah Whately

ADAMS MEDIA

NEW YORK   LONDON   TORONTO   SYDNEY   NEW DELHI

Adams Media
An Imprint of Simon & Schuster, Inc.
100 Technology Center Drive
Stoughton, Massachusetts 02072

An Everything® Series Book.
Everything® and everything.com® are registered trademarks of Simon & Schuster, Inc.

First Adams Media trade paperback edition July 2021

ADAMS MEDIA and colophon are trademarks of Simon & Schuster.

For information about special discounts for bulk purchases, please contact Simon & Schuster Special Sales at 1-866-506-1949 or business@simonandschuster.com.

The Simon & Schuster Speakers Bureau can bring authors to your live event. For more information or to book an event contact the Simon & Schuster Speakers Bureau at 1-866-248-3049 or visit our website at www.simonspeakers.com.

Interior design by Erin Alexander
Illustrations by Jim Steck

Manufactured in the United States of America

Printed by LSC Communications, Crawfordsville, IN, U.S.A.

2 2022

ISBN 978-1-5072-1614-9

Contents

Introduction

Kindergarten-aged children are eager to learn, and math activities during these early years should be fun and engaging. Although they will learn a lot about math with their class, there are many activities that can be done at home to reinforce these all-important skills. Encourage your child to count apples in a bowl, name the shapes of blocks and other toys, and identify patterns all around them. Or take the time to sit together and try some of the colorful, fun, and educational puzzles in *The Everything® Kids' Math Puzzles for Kindergarten*.

This collection of 100 puzzles provides an enjoyable way for your child to practice and develop important early math skills. These puzzles make math fun by using colorful and appealing themes to capture a young child's interest. The book is divided into eight chapters, each focusing on a math topic that corresponds to the US Common Core State Standards. Your child will practice counting, comparing numbers, addition, and subtraction. Later puzzles introduce the concepts of measurement and data, shapes, position, patterns, and position words.

All your child needs are a pencil and some crayons, markers, or colored pencils. And you, of course, to read instructions out loud and encourage your child as they complete the puzzles. Your child will give answers in lots of different ways—by writing a number in a box; drawing a line to the correct answer; or coloring, circling, or putting a checkmark next to an object. They'll be practicing fine motor skills in addition to math.

Each chapter focuses on a different math topic and set of skills. While the puzzles can be done in any order, it's a good idea to move through the ones in Chapters 1 through 6 from beginning to end, because they increase a bit in difficulty. Mix in puzzles from the last two chapters for variety. Here are the things your child will be learning as you work together on the puzzles and activities:

- **Numbers and counting.** These puzzles focus on recognizing and naming numbers and developing counting skills. Your child will solve puzzles by ordering and writing numbers all the way up to 20.
- **Comparing numbers.** In these puzzles your child will look at the numbers to 10 *in relation to each other*. They will compare groups of objects to see which has more, fewer, or the same. They will also compare written numerals.
- **Counting to 100.** In kindergarten, children learn to count all the way up to 100. Fun activities like connect the dots, number mazes, and hundreds charts help them practice ordering all those numbers. You'll also find puzzles that feature skip counting by 10.
- **Adding and subtracting within 10.** Some easier puzzles involve adding and subtracting with the help of pictures, while others involve simple written number sentences or word problems.
- **Measurement and data.** In these puzzles, your child will be looking at different measurable attributes such as length, weight, and capacity. Some puzzles ask your child to sort objects according to their type or properties.
- **Shape, position, and patterns.** In kindergarten, children are introduced to both two-dimensional and three-dimensional shapes. Easy shape puzzles ask your child to identify and name shapes, and more challenging ones direct them to sort shapes according to their attributes. Other puzzles feature shape and color patterns, as well as position words such as *above*, *beside*, and *in front of*.

Don't expect to do too many puzzles in one sitting—a handful of puzzles at a time is best at this age. To help your child get the most out of these puzzles, work through them together. Read the instructions aloud and talk about the math on the page. Encourage your child to use the pictures to help them as they do the puzzles. It may be useful to have something you can count with (such as counters or building blocks) on hand, particularly for the addition and subtraction chapters.

If you come across a puzzle that seems too challenging for your child, that's okay. Leave it and come back to it at another time. At this age, children are developing in leaps and bounds, so a puzzle they may find tricky now will probably seem like a piece of cake later in the kindergarten year. The most important thing is that you and your child have fun working through the book—counting people at the fairground, following a spider maze, or sorting socks. I do hope your child has fun with these puzzles (and learns a bit of math along the way too!).

Chapter 1

Numbers and Counting (Numbers Up to 10)

As you probably already know, young children love counting. In this chapter, there are lots of opportunities to put those counting skills into practice. Your child will count groups of up to 10 objects and order numbers both forward and backward. To help with building number sense, numbers are shown in lots of different ways—in the form of a group of objects, as circles in a ten frame, as tally marks, as dots on dice, or as a written word. It's a lot to learn, but finding underwater creatures, celebrating a birthday, and helping to launch a rocket make it entertaining as well as instructive.

Ice Cream

It's time for ice cream!
Count the dots on the dice, and then use the code to color the picture.

1 = red   2 = pink

3 = yellow   4 = blue

5 = green   6 = brown

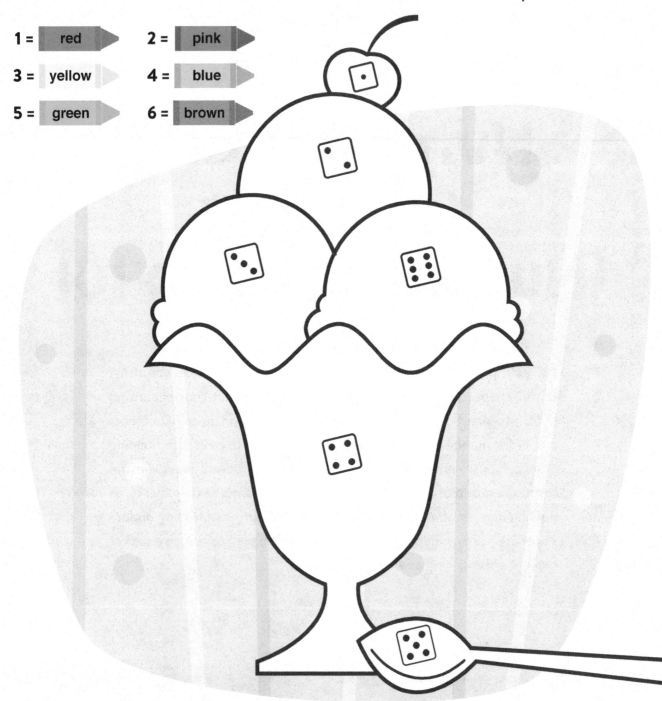

Under the Sea

Can you count the different sea creatures in the picture?
For each type of sea creature, write the number you counted in the box.

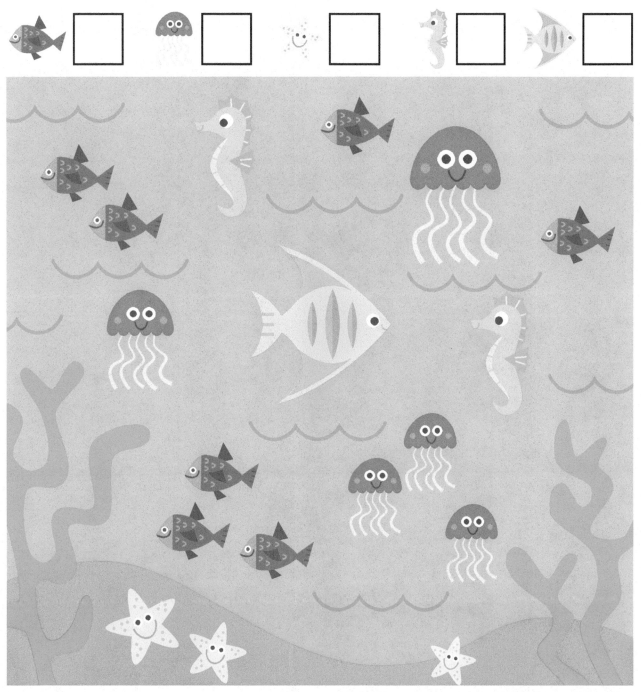

Goldfish Bowls

Put a checkmark (✓) next to the bowls that have **2** fish and **4** bubbles.

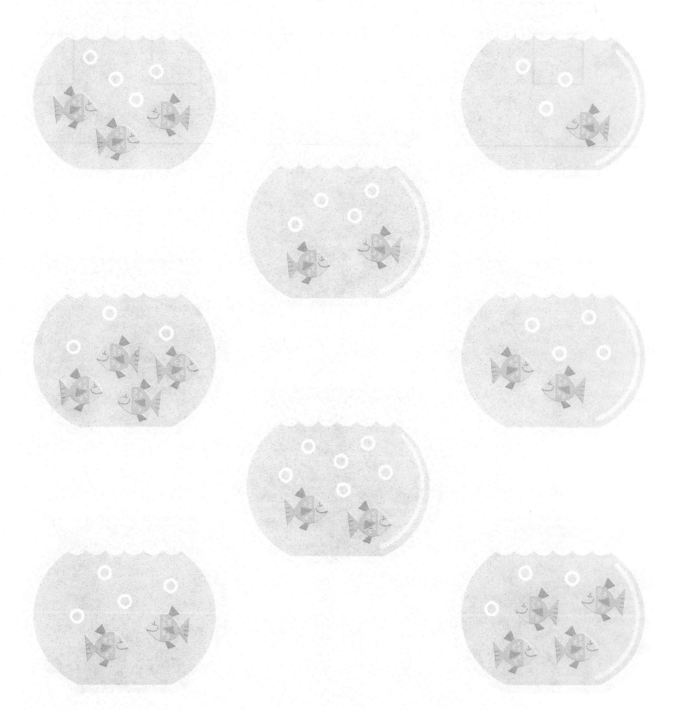

Space Aliens

Here is a space alien from a faraway planet.
Count its eyes, arms, and legs, and then fill in the boxes.

It has ☐ eyes.

It has ☐ arms.

It has ☐ legs.

Can you draw your own space alien in the box? Give your alien **5** eyes, **2** arms, and **3** legs.

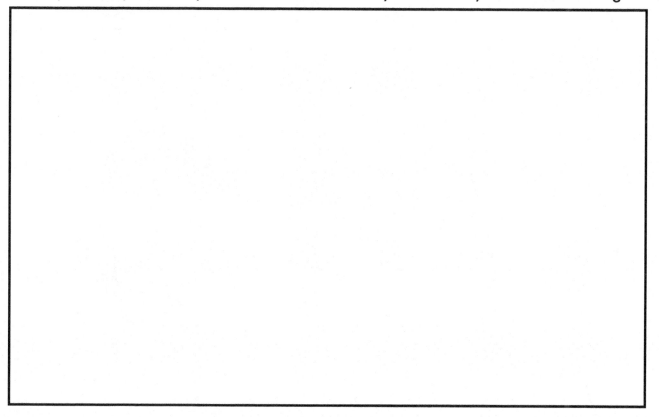

Counting Raindrops

Can you count the raindrops under each cloud? Draw a line to the matching umbrella.

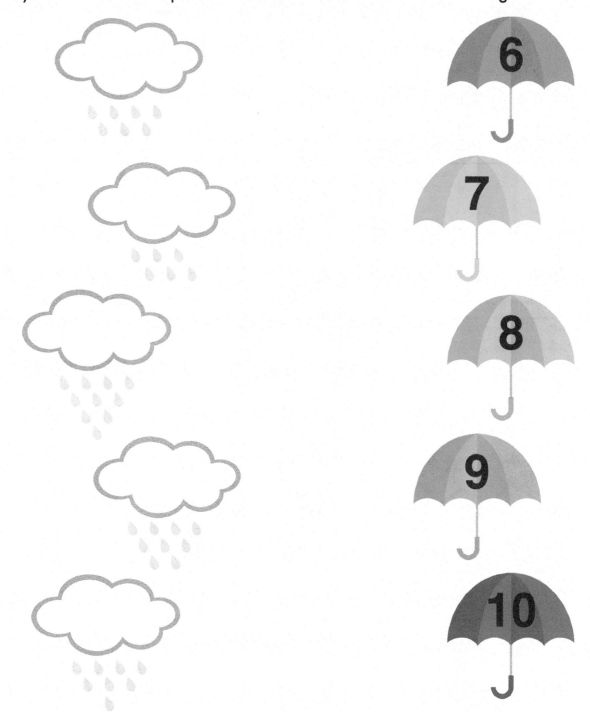

School Buses

Can you count the smiley faces in each school bus?
Write the number you counted in the box.

Draw **5** smiley faces in this bus and color the picture.

Birthday Cake

It's my birthday. I am **6** today!

Can you count the different shapes on the cake and write the number of each shape in the box?

There are ☐ 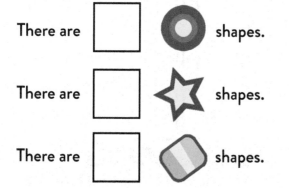 shapes.

There are ☐ ⭐ shapes.

There are ☐ ▱ shapes.

Draw more candles on the cake so that it has **6** altogether.

Ladybugs

Look at the ladybugs on this leaf.

Can you circle the ladybug that does **not** have **7** spots?

Add more spots to this ladybug so it has **7** spots too.

Countdown

Can you help count down from **10** to **1** to launch the rocket?
Fill in the missing numbers.

10

9

7

5

4

2

1

LIFT OFF

Bubbles of 10

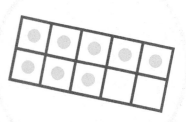

Look at the numbers
shown in the bubbles.

Color all the bubbles
that show **10**.

5

ten

9

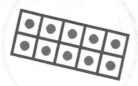

How many bubbles did you color?

Find the Fish

Can you help the cat get to the fish?
Find the path through the maze that follows the numbers **1** to **10** in order.

1	2	3	4	9
2	8	9	5	6
3	4	5	8	3
8	5	6	7	8
3	6	2	1	4
4	7	8	9	10

Scarves

Can you write the missing numbers on these colorful scarves?

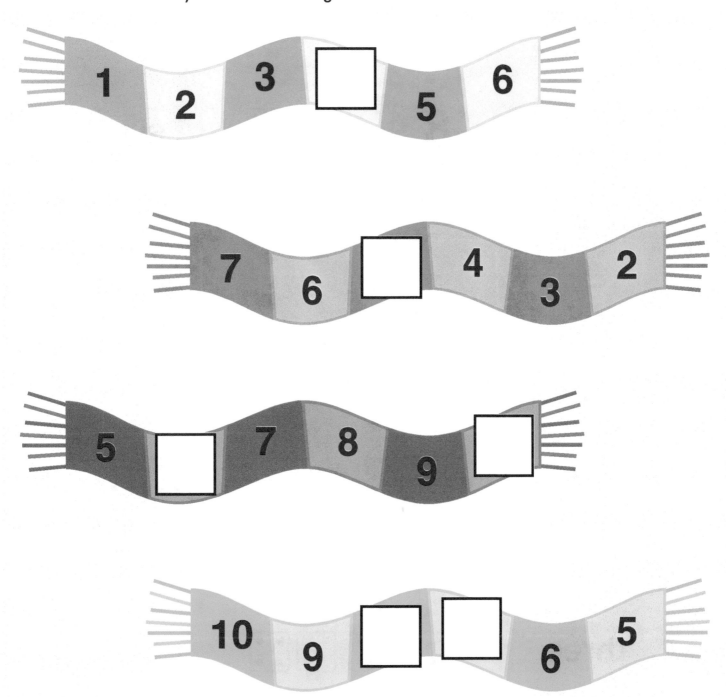

Number Squares (Numbers to 10)

Each row shows four different numbers.
Put a checkmark (✓) under the number you are looking for.

Which square shows **7**?

 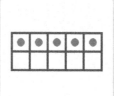  

Which square shows **3**?

Which square shows **10**?

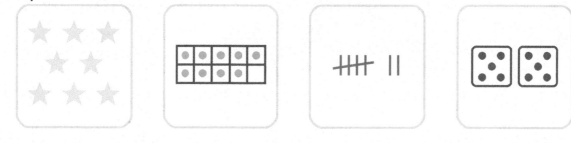

Which square shows **5**?

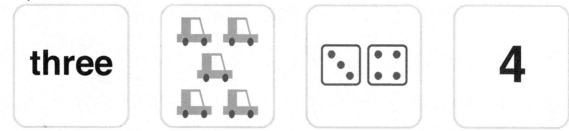

Chapter 2

Numbers and Counting (11-20)

The numbers 11–20 can be tricky to learn. In addition to learning the names of these numbers, your child is also beginning to write numbers that have two digits. As in the 1–10 puzzles, numbers 11 to 20 are shown in a variety of ways—as a group of objects, as a written numeral, or as dots or tally marks. Some of the later puzzles in this chapter incorporate base 10 blocks, which help children to see numbers broken down into 10s and 1s. This collection of puzzles, including connect the dots, mazes, and coded coloring pictures, will help your child continue their counting journey past 10.

On the Farm

Use the code to color the farmyard picture.

11 = green 12 = brown 13 = yellow
14 = blue 15 = pink 16 = red

Balloons

Use red to color all the balloons that show the number **18**.

Color the rest of the balloons using your favorite colors.

Wide Awake

It's nighttime and somebody is wide awake. Starting with **11**, connect the dots in order from **11** to **20** to finish the picture. Then color it in.

How many stars can you count in the night sky?

Bouncy Balls

Bouncy balls are bouncing everywhere! Can you help the girls catch and sort the bouncy balls? Draw a line to match each ball to the correct basket.

Puzzle Pieces

These puzzle pieces are all mixed up!
Count the shapes in each piece, and then draw a line to the correct number.

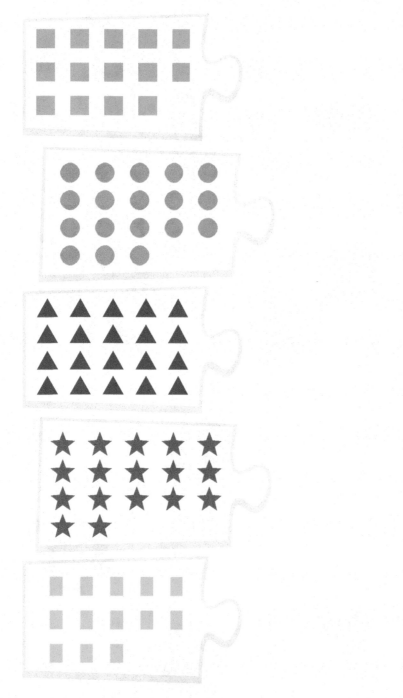

18

20

13

14

17

Which Cheetah?

One of these cheetahs has **12** spots on it. Which one?
When you find it, color it in.

Jack and the Beanstalk

Can you draw **13** leaves on the beanstalk to help Jack climb to the top?

How many magic beans are in my bag?

Spider Maze

Can you find your way through the maze to the spider in the middle?
Follow the numbers in order to get to **20**.

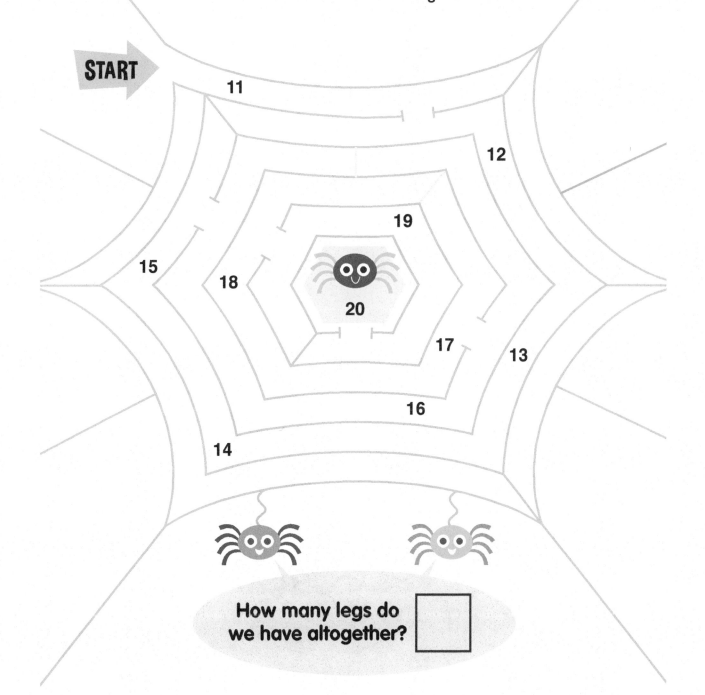

START

11

12

19

15

18

20

17

13

16

14

How many legs do
we have altogether?

Cupcakes

Look at the cupcakes on each tray. Can you fill in the missing numbers?

11　12　13

13　14　　16

15　　17

　　19　20

At the Fairground

Count the people in different parts of the fairground.
Then write the numbers in the boxes.

How many people are
on the Ferris wheel? ☐

How many people are
on the roller coaster?

☐

How many people are on the train? ☐

How many people are waiting for a hot dog? ☐

HOT DOGS

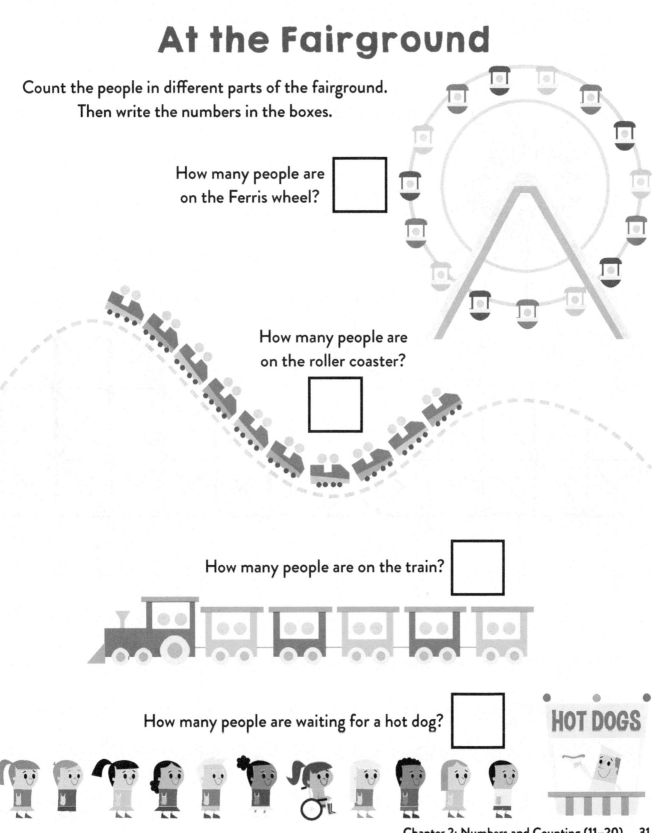

Rainbow Snail

There are some numbers missing from the snail's shell. Can you fill them in?

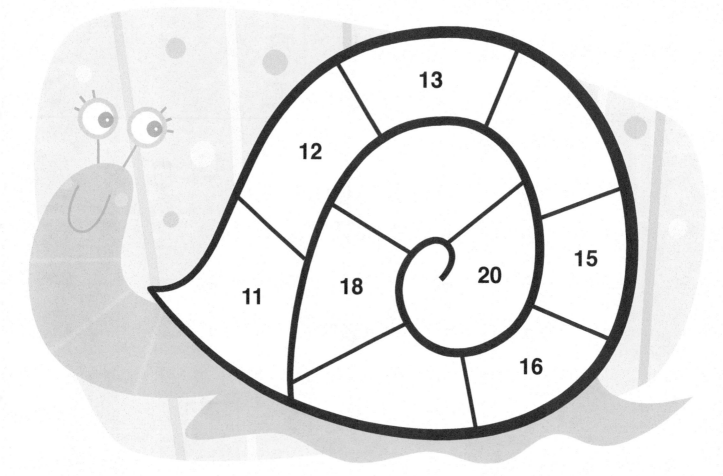

The snail's shell needs some color. Color it using the code.

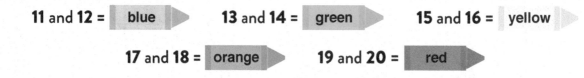

11 and 12 = blue   13 and 14 = green   15 and 16 = yellow

17 and 18 = orange   19 and 20 = red

Flowerpots

Count the blocks on each flowerpot.
Then color the flower with the matching number.

Number Squares (11-20)

Each row shows four different numbers.
Put a checkmark (✓) under the number you are looking for.

Which square shows **16**?

Which square shows **12**?

Which square shows **19**?

Which square shows **14**?

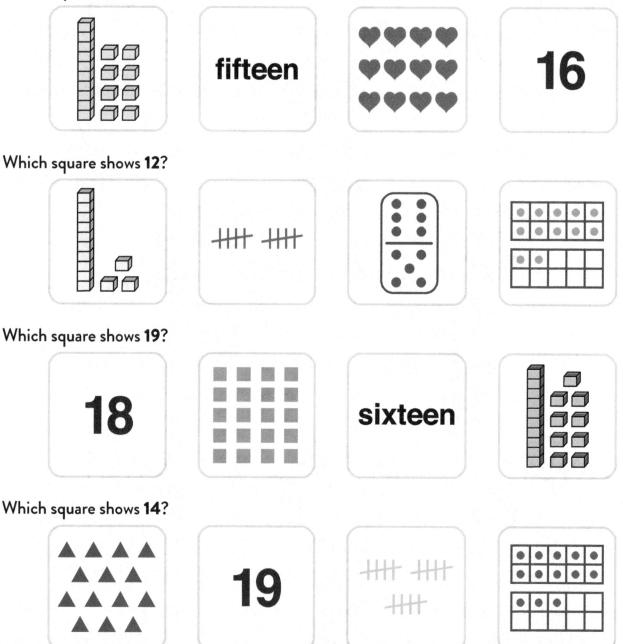

Chapter 3

Comparing Numbers

The puzzles in this chapter focus on comparing numbers. Your child will compare numbers up to 10 in the form of both numerals and groups of objects. By comparing the number of shells on sandcastles, spots on butterflies, or spikes on dinosaurs, your child will become familiar with terms such as *more than*, *less than*, *most*, *fewest*, and *same*. Some of the puzzles introduce the written symbols for *greater than* (>) and *less than* (<) as well as the *equal sign* (=).

Sandcastles

Draw lines to connect the sandcastles that have the **same** number of shells.

Peapods

Can you circle the peapods that have **more than 4** peas?

Butterflies

Here are two butterflies.

Can you decorate this butterfly so that it has **more** spots than its colorful friend?

Watermelon Seeds

Can you circle the watermelon slices that have **less than 8** seeds?

Which Dog?

Here are four dogs and four children. Draw a line to match each child to their pet dog.

My dog has 3 spots.

My dog has more than 6 spots.

My dog has less than 3 spots.

My dog has 5 spots.

Dinosaurs

Here are two dinosaurs.

Draw **6 more** spikes on this dinosaur.

Draw **5 more** spikes on this dinosaur.

Now count how many spikes each dinosaur has altogether.

Which dinosaur has **more** spikes? Color it green

Which dinosaur has **fewer** spikes? Color it orange

Number Pies

Here are four freshly baked number pies.
For each pie, write the **smallest** number in the box underneath.

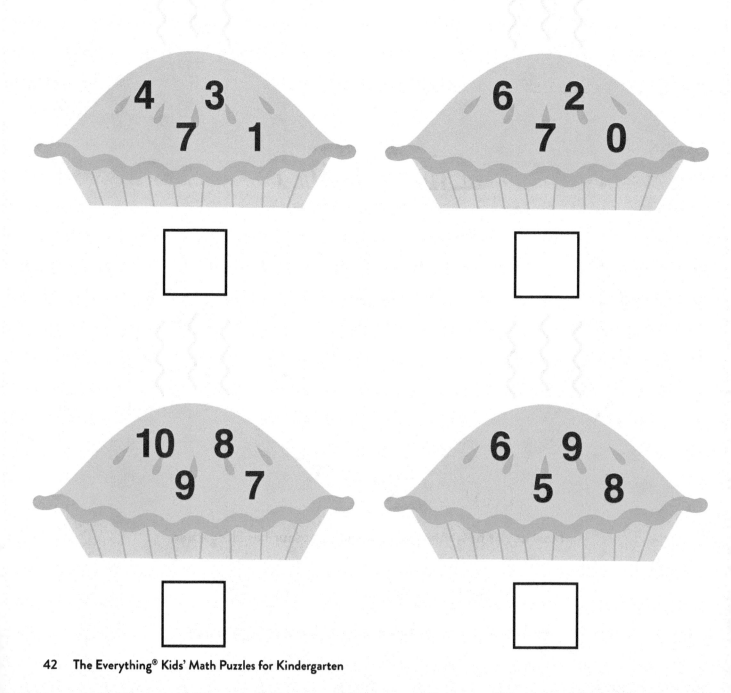

Crocodiles

For each pair of numbers, circle the correct crocodile.
(And remember: The hungry crocodile always eats the **bigger** number.)

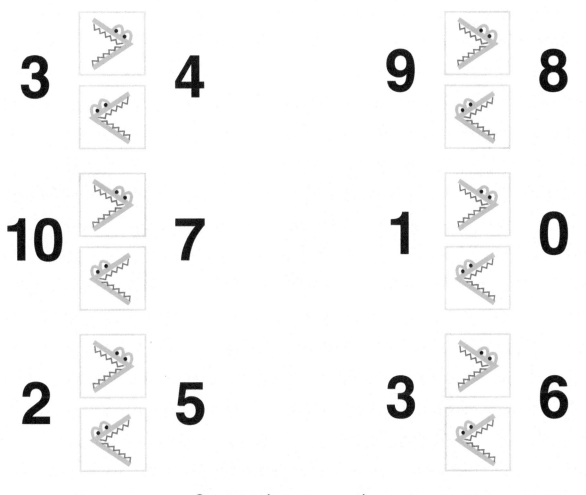

3   4   9   8

10   7   1   0

2   5   3   6

Compare these two numbers.
Can you draw your own crocodile symbol in the box?

8   6

Pizzas

Can you count and compare the number of mushrooms on each pair of pizzas?
Write **>**, **<**, or **=** in each box.

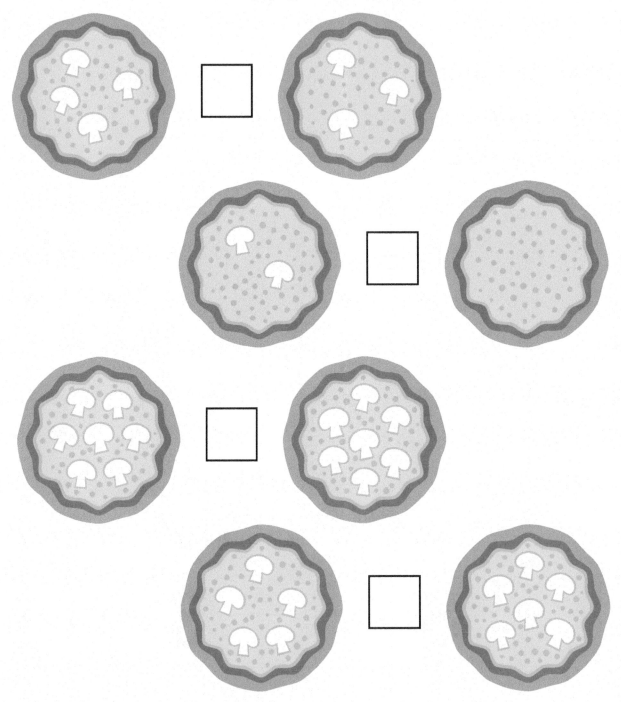

Marbles

Here are two jars full of colored marbles. Answer each question by coloring either **A** or **B**.

Which jar has **more** ● ? (A) (B)

Which jar has **more** ● ? (A) (B)

Which jar has **more** ● ? (A) (B)

Which jar has **more** ● ? (A) (B)

Storming the Castle

Look carefully at the picture. Are there more people **inside** the castle or **outside** the castle? Put a checkmark (✓) in the correct box.

There are more people:

inside the castle [ ]   **outside** the castle [ ]

Apples

Look at the number sentences in the apples. Some are **true** and some are **false**.
Can you color the ones that are **true**?

6 > 4

4 < 3

4 = 4

10 < 7

9 > 8

0 < 3

2 = 3

8 > 5

Chapter 4

Counting to 100

In this chapter, your child will have lots of practice at counting to 100. They will join numbers in order, find missing numbers, and decide what number should come next in a counting sequence. Some of the puzzles show a group of numbers at a time (for example, 20–30 or 40–60), while others use a hundreds chart so that children can see all numbers to 100 at once. At the end of this chapter, you will find puzzles that practice skip counting by 10—in one instance, by way of a group of party-loving penguins.

Houses

Look at the houses on the street.
Use the numbers on the front doors to help you answer the questions.

Which number
comes after **22**?

Which number
comes before **30**?

Which number
comes after **24**?

Which number
comes before **21**?

Which number
comes after **29**?

Polly

Connect the dots in counting order from **1** to **35** to see who is sitting on the captain's shoulder.

Then color the picture.

Trains

Look at the numbers on each train.
Can you draw a line to the number that comes next?

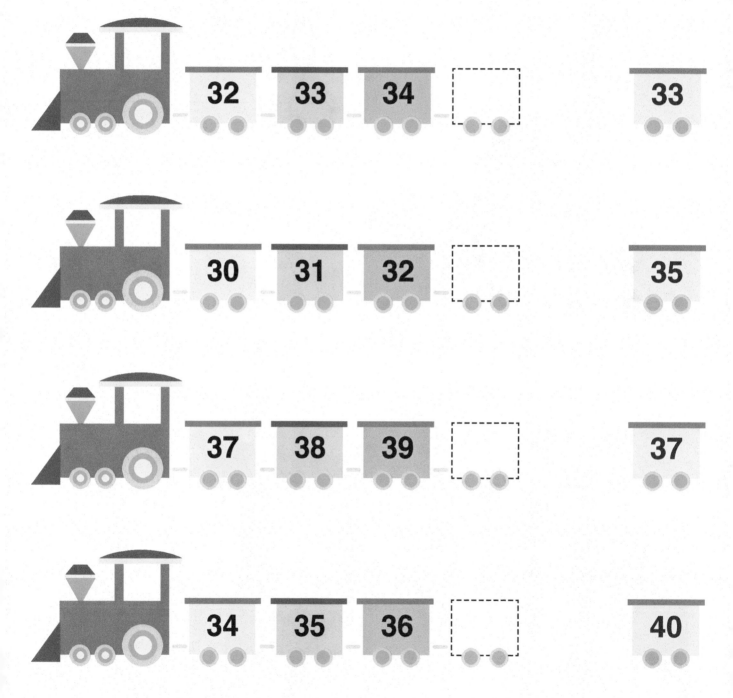

Caterpillars

Can you write the last number on each colorful caterpillar?

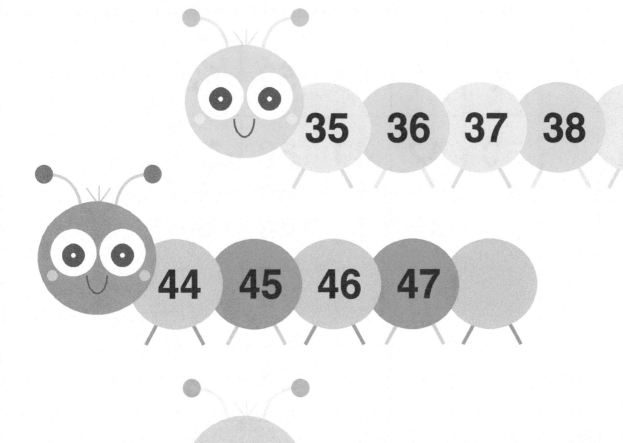

35 36 37 38

44 45 46 47

59 60 61 62

66 67 68 69

Bird's Nest

Which nest does the bird live in? Find the bird's home by following the numbers in order from **40** to **60**. Color the nest to show your answer.

40	41	45	53	52
50	42	49	50	51
59	43	44	45	46
51	50	49	48	47
52	53	54	44	58
48	49	55	56	59
60	59	58	57	60

What's My Name?

Color these numbers on the hundreds chart to find out the missing letter of the girl's name:
14, 15, 16, 17, 18, 26, 36, 46, 54, 56, 64, 65, 66. Write the letter on the line.

1	2	3	4	5	6	7	8	9	10
11	12	13	14	15	16	17	18	19	20
21	22	23	24	25	26	27	28	29	30
31	32	33	34	35	36	37	38	39	40
41	42	43	44	45	46	47	48	49	50
51	52	53	54	55	56	57	58	59	60
61	62	63	64	65	66	67	68	69	70
71	72	73	74	75	76	77	78	79	80
81	82	83	84	85	86	87	88	89	90
91	92	93	94	95	96	97	98	99	100

My name is

____ess

Up in the Sky

Can you connect the dots to find out what is flying in the sky?
Start at **50** and count all the way to **70**. Then color the picture.

Paint Splatters

Oh, no! I've spilled paint on my page. Can you work out which numbers have been covered up? Write the missing numbers on the paint splatters.

1	2	3	4	5	6	7	8	9	10
11	12		14	15	16	17	18	19	20
21	22	23	24	25	26	27	28	29	30
31	32	33	34	35	36	37	38	39	40
	42	43	44	45	46	47	48	49	50
51	52	53	54	55		57	58	59	60
61	62	63	64	65	66	67	68	69	70
71	72	73	74	75	76	77	78	79	80
81		83	84	85	86	87	88	89	
91	92	93	94	95	96	97	98	99	100

Who's Swimming?

Connect the dots to see who is jumping out of the water.
Start at **70** and count all the way to **100**. Then color the picture.

Counting Crayons

Each box has **10** crayons inside. For each group of boxes, count by **10** to see how many crayons there are altogether. Color the correct answer.

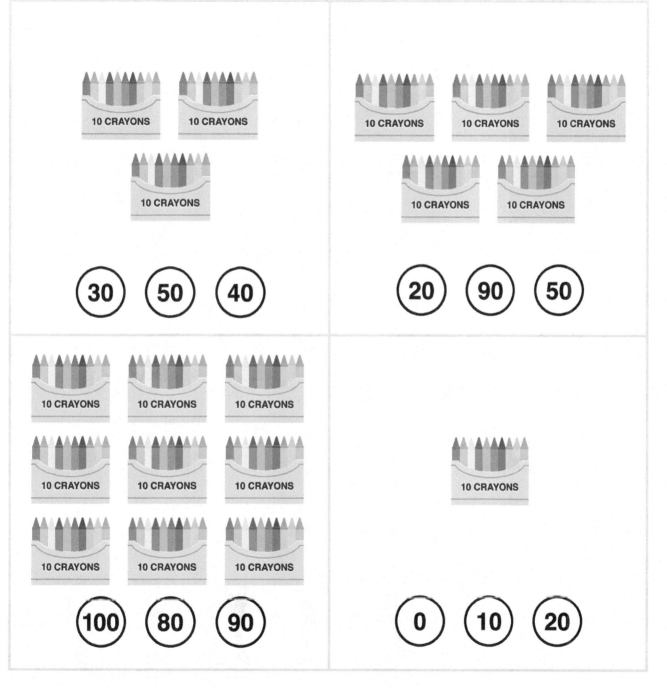

Party Penguins

The penguins are having a party!
Write the missing numbers on the penguins' party hats as you count by **10**.

10 → 20 → __ → 40

50

__

__

80 → __ → 100

How many
penguin feet are
there altogether?

Jumping Frog

Can you count by **10** to help the frog find the fly?
Starting at **10**, draw a line to show the correct path across the lily pads to **100**.

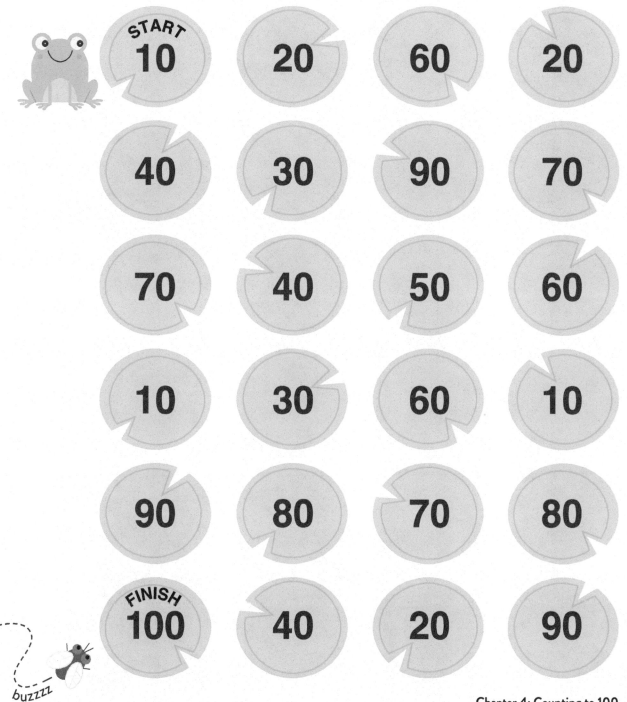

START
10

20

60

20

40

30

90

70

70

40

50

60

10

30

60

10

90

80

70

80

FINISH
100

40

20

90

buzzzz

Chapter 5

Adding

At this age, children are introduced to addition as the idea of *putting numbers together*. You can help reinforce this concept with everyday practice using whatever is around you—toy cars, counters, or cookies on a plate. And puzzles add to the fun and learning. They start with addition within 5 before progressing to addition within 10. Here, you'll find picture addition puzzles (adding together groups of objects), number sentences, and simple word problems. Remind your child to use the pictures to help them with the puzzles. You could also have physical objects like blocks or pebbles on hand to count with.

Ducklings

Count the ducklings in each group. Add them together and write the number in the box.

Which Carrot?

Can you draw a line to match each rabbit to the correct carrot?

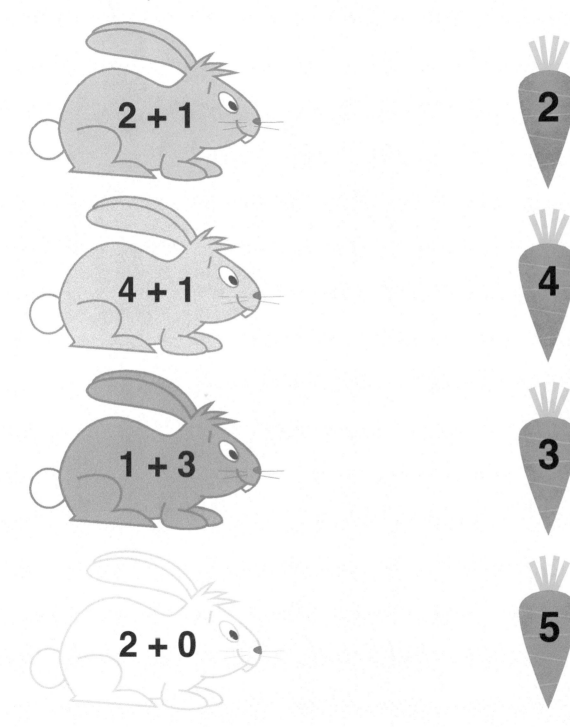

2 + 1

4 + 1

1 + 3

2 + 0

2

4

3

5

Sunflower

This sunflower has lots of leaves. Can you find the leaves with numbers that add up to **5**.

Color them **green**

3 + 2

4 + 2

3 + 1

1 + 4

5 + 0

Let's Play!

Count the balls in each group. Add them together and color the correct answer.

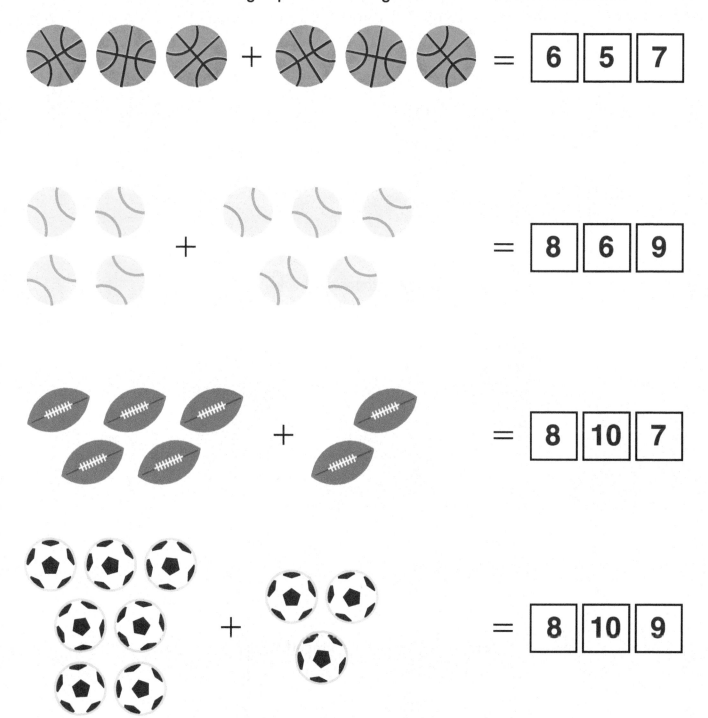

Library Books

At the library, I choose **4** books.

My sister chooses **5** books.

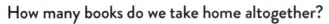

How many books do we take home altogether?

In the Rainforest

Who's sitting on the branch?
Solve the addition questions, and then use the code to color the picture.

1 = yellow   2 = white   3 = orange

4 = black   5 = green   6 = blue

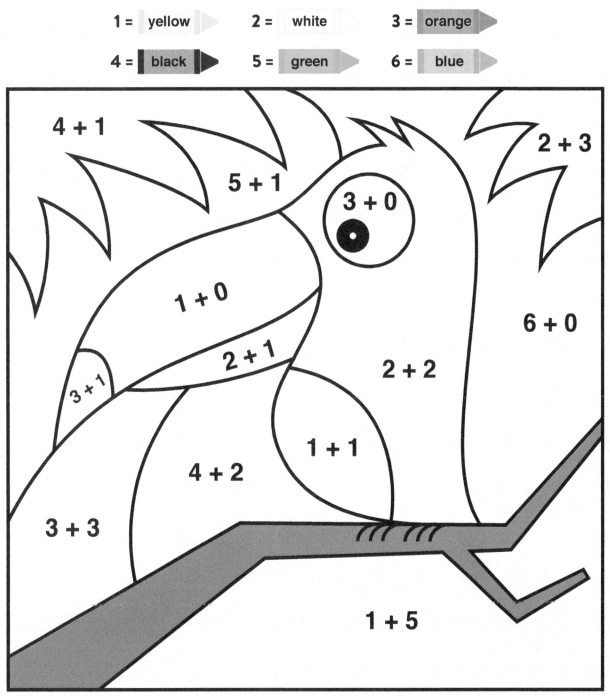

Dice

Add together the two numbers shown on the dice.
Then draw a line to the correct answer.

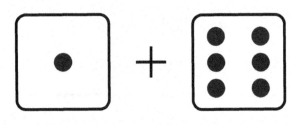

 +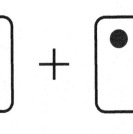

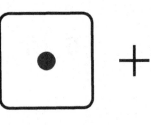

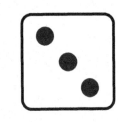

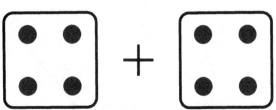

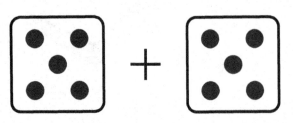

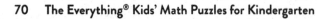

Hamburgers

There should be **10** hamburgers on my tray, but my dog keeps taking them when I'm not looking!

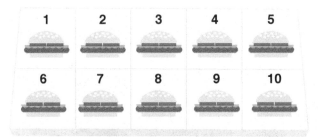

For each tray below, count the hamburgers and write how many are missing.

There are ☐ 🍔
There are ☐ missing

There are ☐ 🍔
There are ☐ missing

There are ☐ 🍔
There are ☐ missing

There are ☐ 🍔
There are ☐ missing

Strawberry Picking

Can you add together the numbers on each strawberry?
Draw a line to match each strawberry to the correct basket.

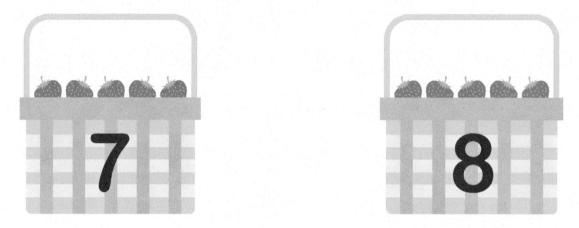

Twins

Here are five sets of twins. For each pair, can you make the numbers on the T-shirts add up to **10**? Fill in the number that's missing.

Hot-Air Balloons

Look at all the hot-air balloons.
Can you color all the hot-air balloons that add up to the number **9**?

6 + 3

4 + 4

2 + 7

5 + 5

1 + 8

4 + 5

How many birds can
you count in the sky?

Chapter 6

Subtracting

As with addition, you can help your child learn the concept of subtraction using everyday items. In this chapter, your child will enjoy picture puzzles, puzzles with number sentences, and simple word problems. Themes like squirrels, the beach, and honey-loving bears make subtraction practice fun. When doing the picture puzzles, encourage your child to use the pictures to help them find their answer (for example, by crossing out the amount that is being subtracted). Also, you might find it helpful to use small objects to help reinforce the idea of *taking away*.

Fruit Salad

Cross out pieces of fruit to help you finish each number sentence.
Write your answer in the box.

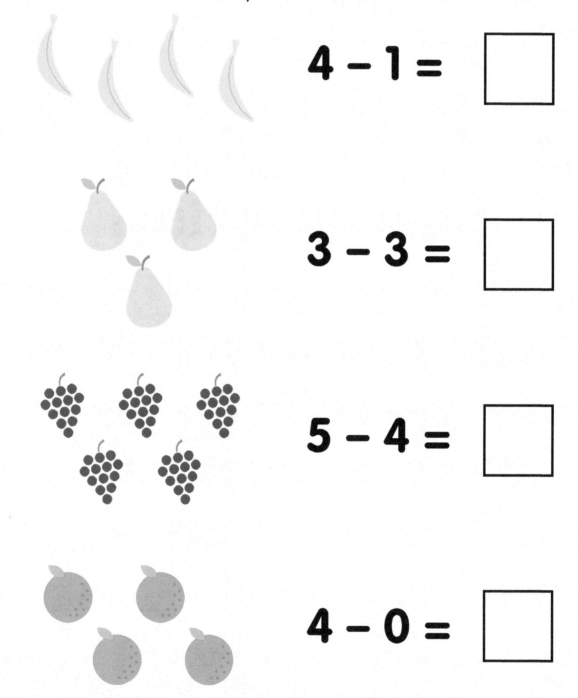

4 − 1 = ☐

3 − 3 = ☐

5 − 4 = ☐

4 − 0 = ☐

At the Bakery

There are **5** loaves of bread for sale at the bakery.

A customer buys **2** loaves.

How many loaves are left? ☐

What treat do you like from the bakery? Draw it on the empty plate.

Hats

Look at all the different hats. Put a checkmark (✓)
next to all the hats that have the answer **2**.

4 − 2

5 − 3

3 − 2

4 − 0

2 − 2

3 − 1

Squirrels

Can you draw a line to match each squirrel to the correct acorn?

Bears and Honey

These bears are hungry! For each question, cross out the number of honey jars the bear has eaten. Then write how many jars are left in the box.

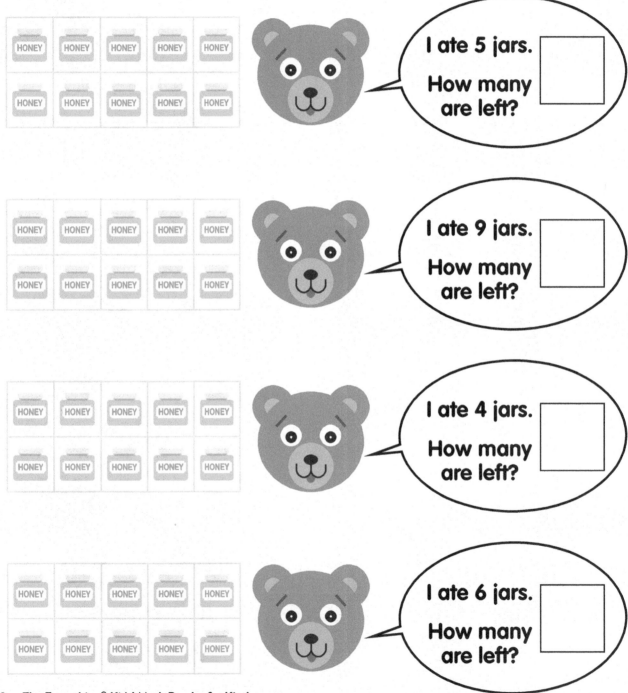

I ate 5 jars.

How many are left?

I ate 9 jars.

How many are left?

I ate 4 jars.

How many are left?

I ate 6 jars.

How many are left?

Bees

There are **7** bees near the hive.

3 bees fly away to collect some pollen.

How many bees are left?

Fishing

This girl is busy fishing.

Can you color all the fish that have the answer **4**?

On the Beach

It's a beautiful day at the beach.
Answer the subtraction questions, and then use the code to color the beach objects.

1 = orange 2 = green 3 = blue

4 = red 5 = purple 6 = yellow

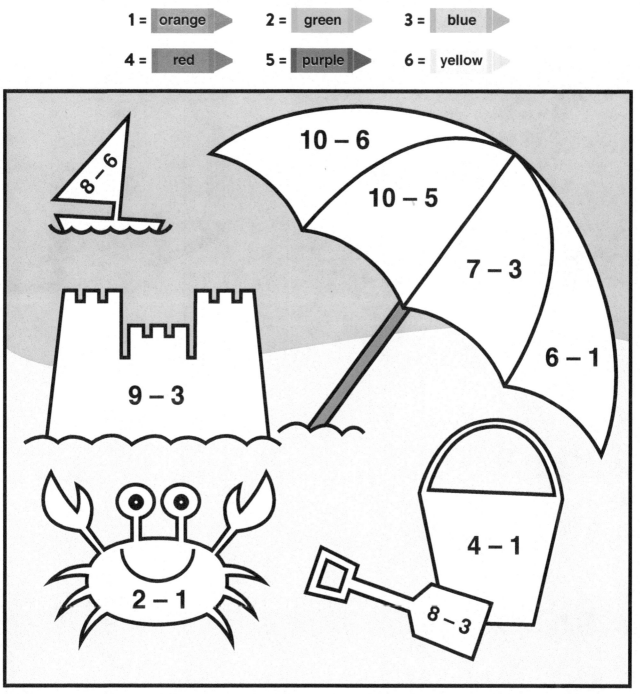

Flying Saucers

Can you draw a line to match each flying saucer to the correct planet?

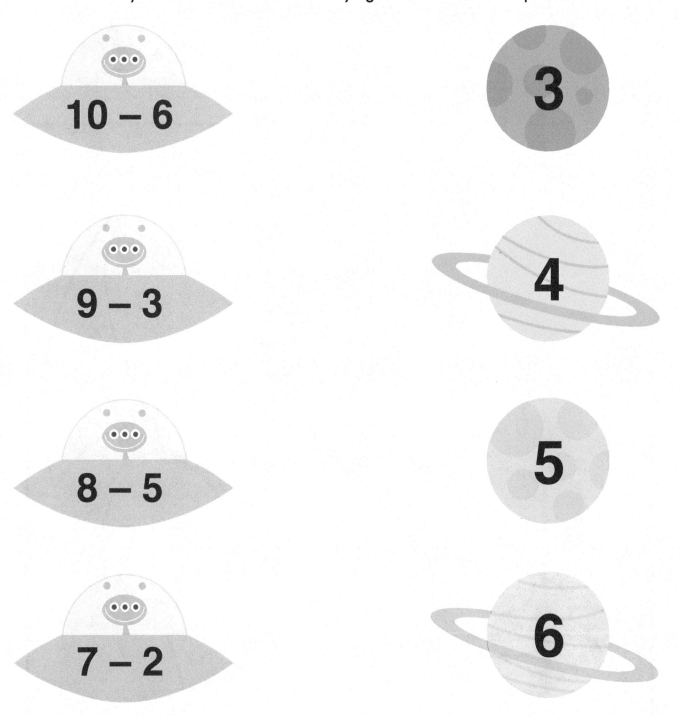

10 – 6

9 – 3

8 – 5

7 – 2

3

4

5

6

Happy or Sad?

Look at these number sentences. Some of them are right and some are wrong.
If the number sentence is right, color the happy face. If it is wrong, color the sad face.

$10 - 3 = 6$

$9 - 6 = 3$

$8 - 6 = 4$

$9 - 1 = 8$

$10 - 8 = 2$

Chapter 7

Measurement and Data

Measurement puzzles focus on attributes such as height, length, width, and capacity. These activities will help your child practice comparing two (or sometimes more) objects in terms of these attributes. For example, they may have to decide which wiggly worm is longer, which backyard object is heavier, or which snowman is the tallest. This chapter will also give your child practice at sorting things according to their properties, such as size, color, or number of legs.

Which Animal?

Can you draw a line to match each description to the correct animal?

This animal is tall with a long neck.

This animal is small and light.

This animal is big and heavy.

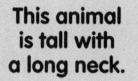

Sorting Socks

Can you help sort the socks?

Color the socks with spots **blue** ▶   Color the socks with stripes **yellow** ▶

How many **blue** socks are there? ☐

How many **yellow** socks are there? ☐

Legs

Can you sort these creatures into those that have **4** legs and those that don't?
Draw a line from each creature to the correct label.

Has 4 legs

Does not
have 4 legs

Snowmen

Look at the three cheery snowmen.
Answer the questions below by writing **A**, **B**, or **C** in the box.

Which snowman is the **tallest**?

Which snowman is the **shortest**?

Which snowman has the **most** buttons?

Which snowman has the **biggest** hat?

In the Backyard

For each pair of objects, can you circle the one that would be **heavier**?

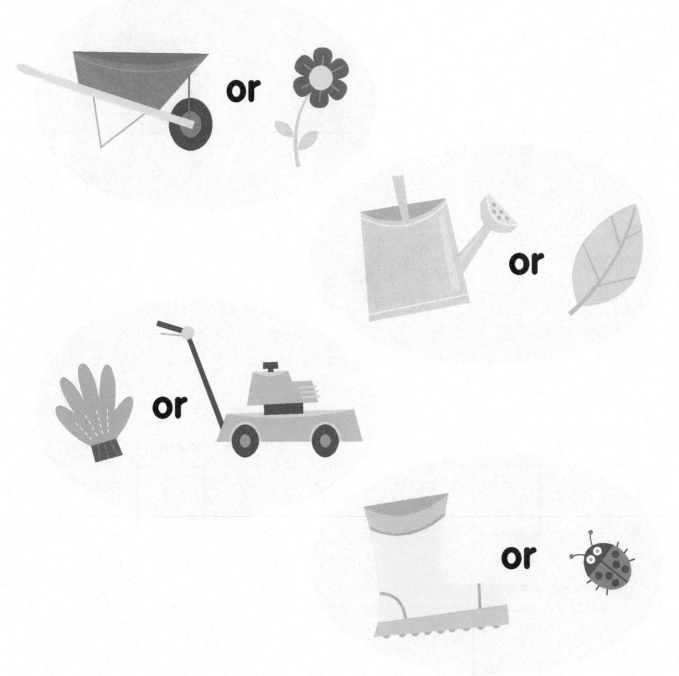

Pairs

Here are four pairs of objects. For each pair, can you put a checkmark (✓) next to the one that is **shorter**?

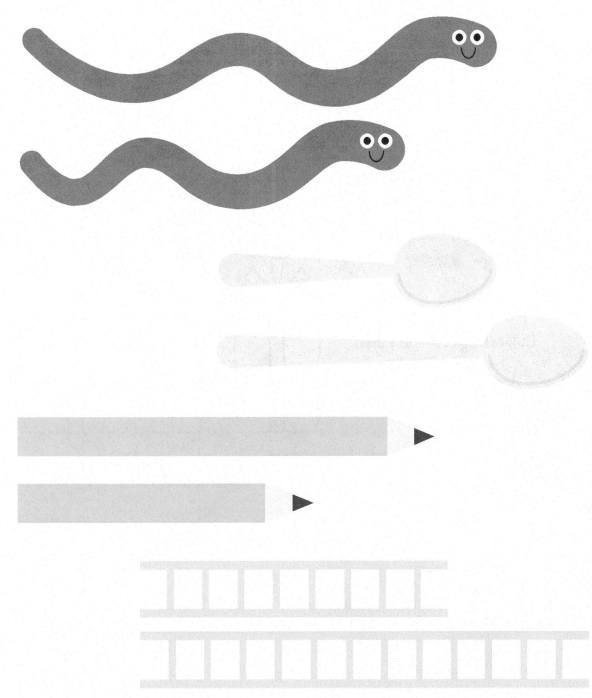

Gifts

Look at each set of gifts. For each question, color your answer.

Color the gift that is **widest**.

Color the gift that is **tallest**.

Color the gift that is **smallest**.

On the Move

The pictures on this page show different ways of getting from one place to another. Some of the pictures show things with wheels and some show things without wheels.

Circle the things **with wheels** in green ▶ Circle the things **with no wheels** in red ▶

Pencil Case

Can you count how many blocks long each object is?

Put a checkmark (✓) next to the **longest** object.

Put a smiley face 🙂 next to the **shortest** object.

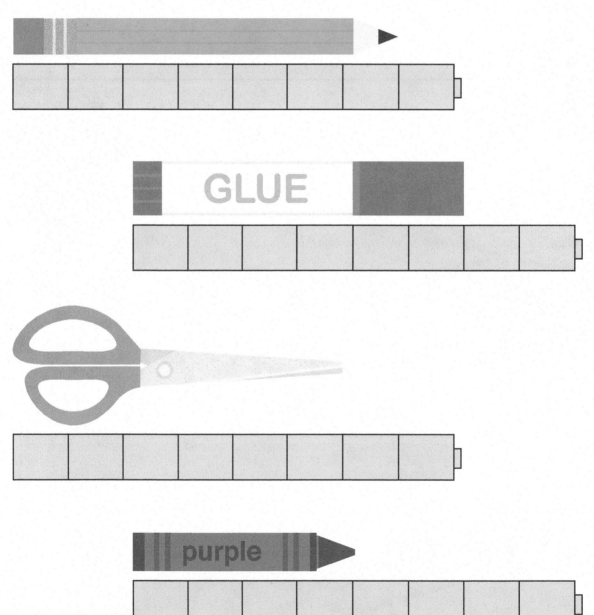

Enchanted Forest

Look at all the toadstools in the enchanted forest.

Color the **big** toadstools red ▶   Color the **small** toadstools purple ▶

Are there more red or purple toadstools?
Check the correct box.

Water

Look at the three containers on the table.
Answer the questions by writing **A**, **B**, or **C** in the box.

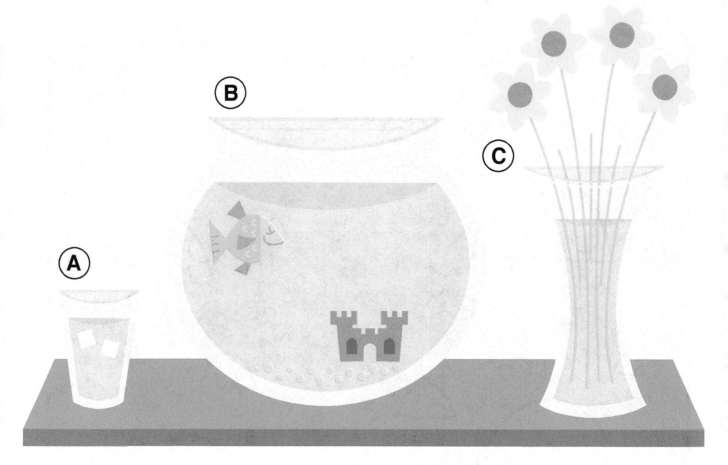

Which container holds the **most** water?

Which container holds the **least** water?

Can you add **1** more ice cube, **2** more fish, and **3** more flowers to the picture?

How's the Weather?

The clothes have been sorted into two groups: warm weather clothes and cold weather clothes. Unfortunately, there are some mistakes. Can you circle the clothes that are in the wrong group?

Jelly Beans

Can you count the different colored jelly beans?
Color the blocks on the chart to show how many of each color there are.

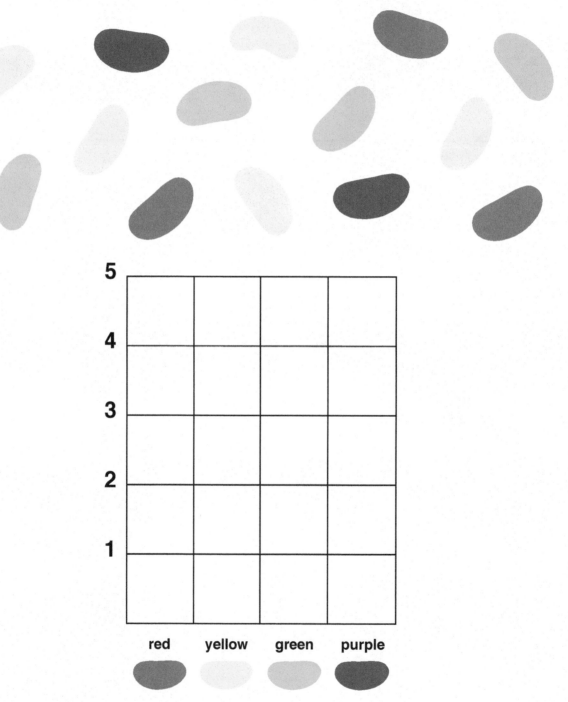

Chapter 8

Shapes and Patterns

The shape puzzles in this chapter feature both two-dimensional (2-D) and three-dimensional (3-D) shapes. Your child will practice identifying and naming these shapes, spotting them in different scenarios, and sorting them according to their type and properties (such as number of sides, faces, or corners). In addition to shape puzzles, this chapter includes puzzles about position words (such as *in front of*, *next to*, and *inside*). Pattern puzzles ask your child to continue or complete simple repeating patterns made with shapes and colors.

Everyday Shapes

Can you draw a line to match each object to the correct shape?

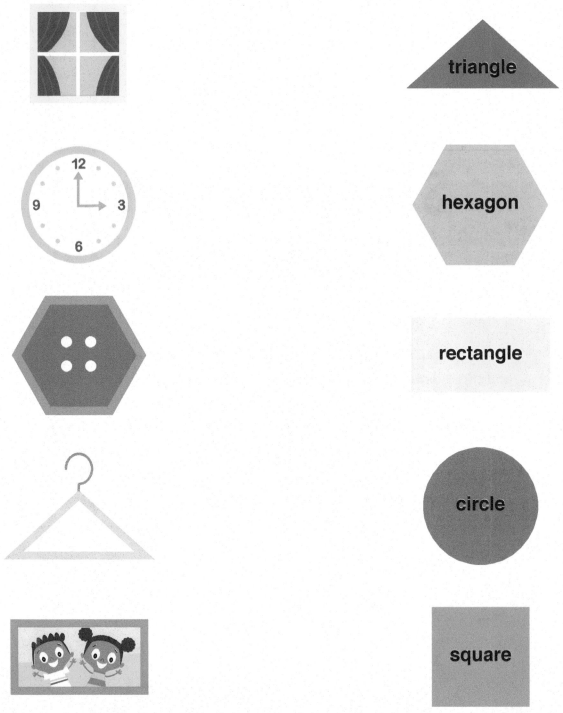

triangle

hexagon

rectangle

circle

square

Mice and Cheese

Mice love cheese! For each row, circle the picture that matches the sentence.

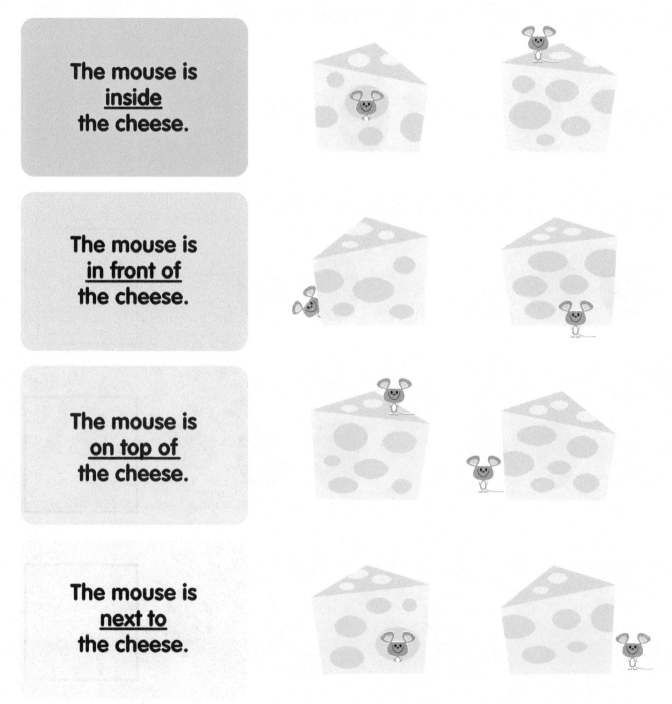

The mouse is <u>inside</u> the cheese.

The mouse is <u>in front of</u> the cheese.

The mouse is <u>on top of</u> the cheese.

The mouse is <u>next to</u> the cheese.

Jewels

Look at the patterns made by the sparkly jewels.
For each pattern, can you draw the shape that comes next?

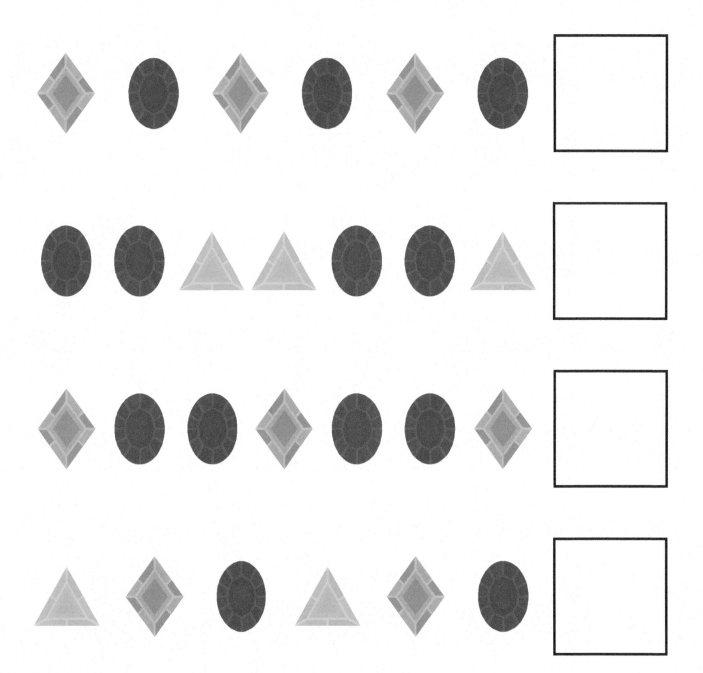

Design a Hat

Can you decorate this hat using shapes? Color it to make it bright and colorful.

Can you use these shapes in your design?

Kites

Look at the shapes on the children's kites.
Match each kite to the correct child by writing **A**, **B**, **C**, or **D** in each box.

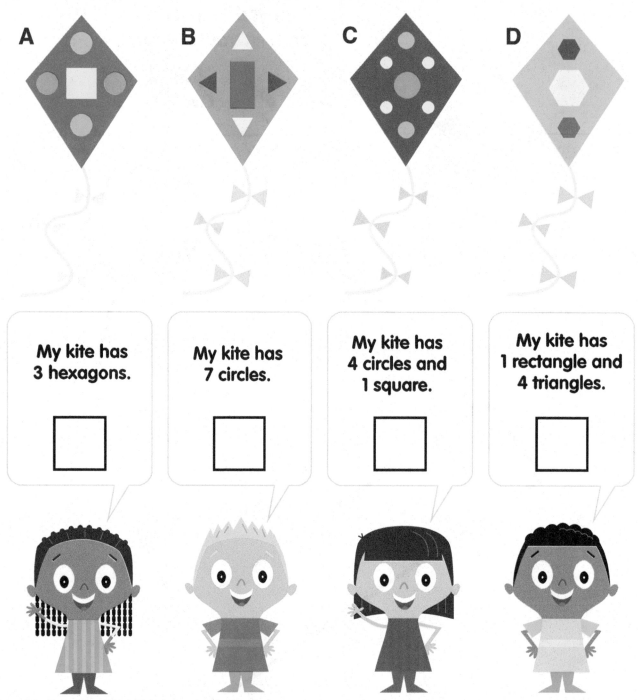

A

B

C

D

My kite has
3 hexagons.

My kite has
7 circles.

My kite has
4 circles and
1 square.

My kite has
1 rectangle and
4 triangles.

Robot

This robot is made of different shapes.

Color the **rectangles**　blue

Color the **triangles**　red

Color the **hexagons**　yellow

Can you count the different shapes? Write the numbers in the boxes.

rectangles　　　**triangles**　　　**hexagons**

Cookies

These children want to tell you about their cookies.
Look at each cookie on the tray, and write **A**, **B**, **C**, or **D** in each box.

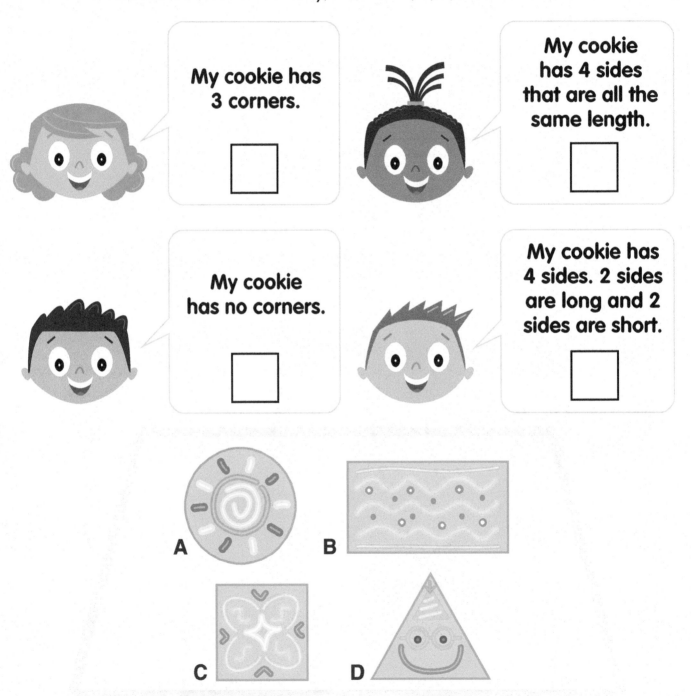

My cookie has 3 corners.

My cookie has 4 sides that are all the same length.

My cookie has no corners.

My cookie has 4 sides. 2 sides are long and 2 sides are short.

A

B

C

D

Shape Pictures

Shapes can join together to make pictures.
Draw a line to match each picture to the shapes you would need to build it.

Pictures

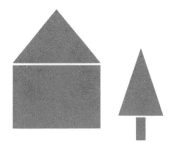

Shapes

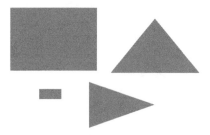

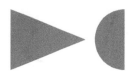

Flat or Solid?

Some of these shapes are **flat** (2-D) and some are **solid** (3-D).

Color all the **flat** shapes [red] ▶   Color all the **solid** shapes [blue] ▶

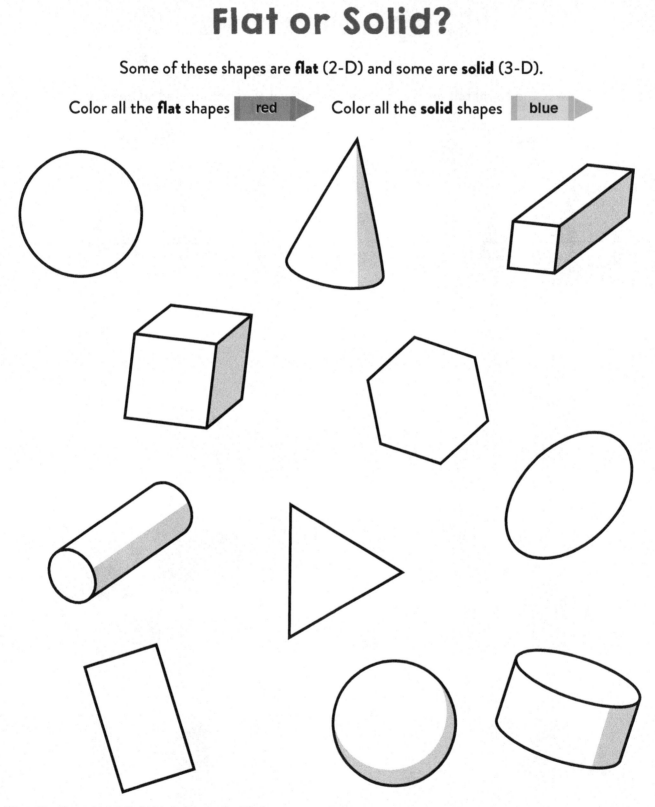

Shape People

Look at these shape people. They are each a different solid shape.
Can you draw a line to match each shape person to the correct shape name?

sphere

cylinder

cone

cube

Traffic Light

Look at the long line of cars waiting at the red light.
Continue the color pattern by coloring the last four cars.

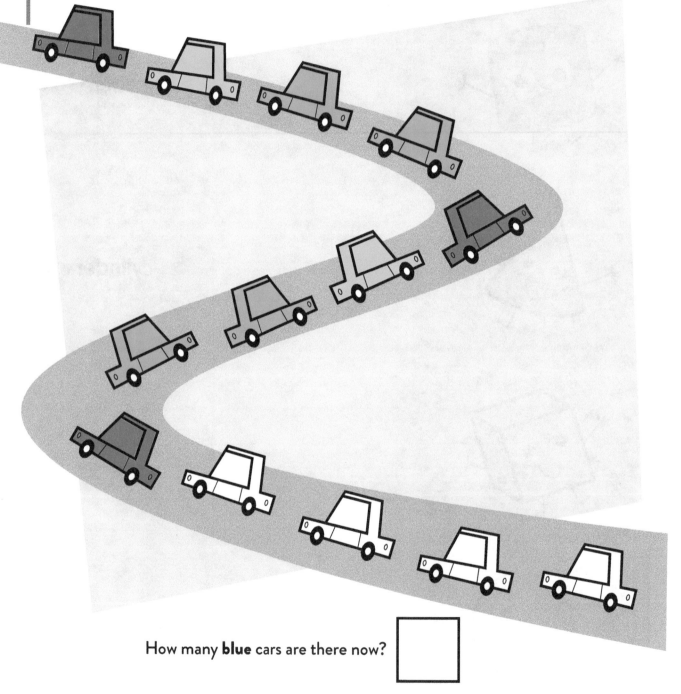

How many **blue** cars are there now?

Shapes All Around

This boy is busy drawing a picture. Look at the objects around his room. There are a lot of solid shapes to spot. Find and circle:

5 cylinders red   **3** spheres blue   **4** cubes green

Toy Store

Look at the toys on the shelves.
For each sentence, color the box that makes the sentence true.

The 🧸 is | in front of / beside | the 🪀

The 🏐 is | above / below | the 👧

The ✈️ is | behind / beside | the 🎸

The 🦖 is | below / above | the 🪀

There is a mouse hiding **behind** one of the toys. Can you spot it and circle it?

What Am I?

For each clue, can you circle the correct shape?

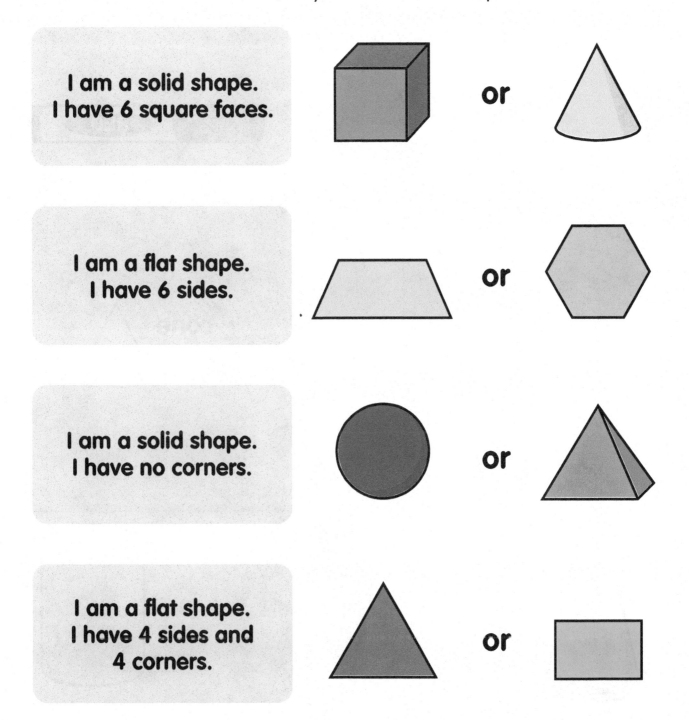

I am a solid shape.
I have 6 square faces.

or

I am a flat shape.
I have 6 sides.

or

I am a solid shape.
I have no corners.

or

I am a flat shape.
I have 4 sides and
4 corners.

or

Cone or Cylinder?

Can you sort the shapes into **cones** and **cylinders**?
Draw a line to match each shape to the correct shape name.

cylinder

cone

What Is Missing?

Look at the four different shape patterns. In each pattern,
there is a **?** where a shape is missing. Can you circle the missing shape?

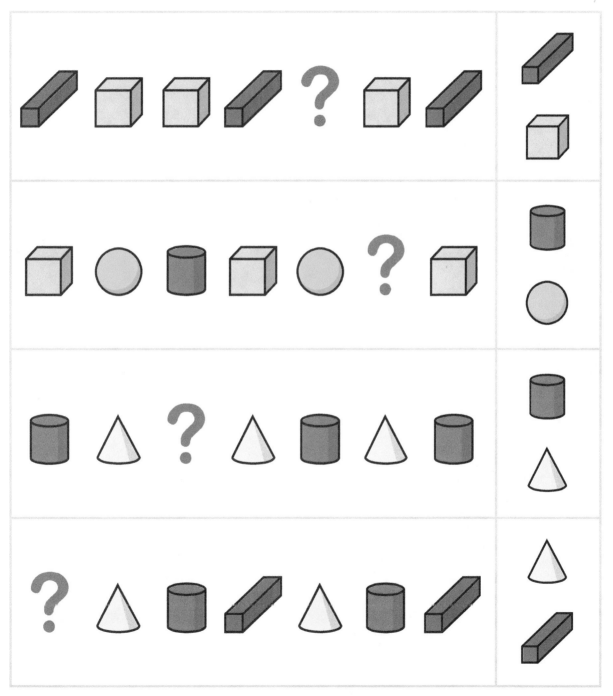

Answers

Chapter 1

Page 8 • Ice Cream

Page 9 • Under the Sea

Page 10 • Goldfish Bowls

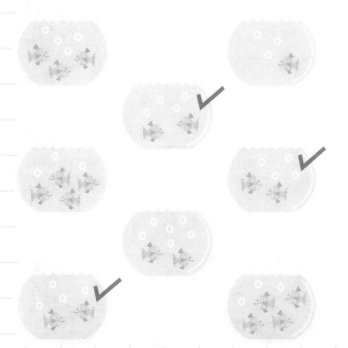

Page 11 • Space Aliens

Page 12 • Counting Raindrops

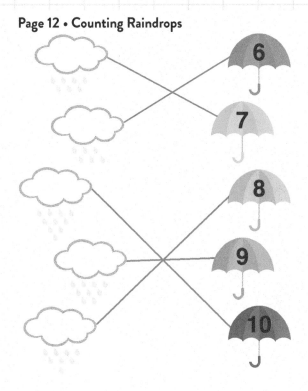

Page 13 • School Buses

Page 14 • Birthday Cake

Page 15 • Ladybugs

Page 16 • Countdown

10
9
8
7
6
5
4
3
2
1

LIFT OFF

Page 17 • Bubbles of 10

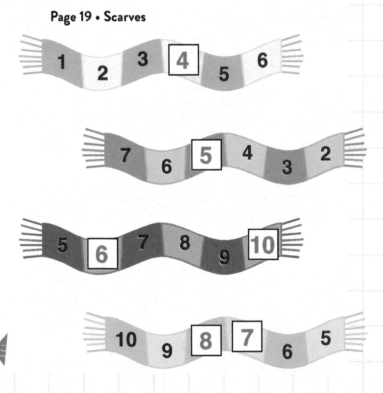

5

ten

9

10

6

Page 18 • Find the Fish

1	2	3	4	9
2	8	9	5	6
3	4	5	8	3
8	5	6	7	8
3	6	2	1	4
4	7	8	9	10

Page 19 • Scarves

1 2 3 4 5 6

7 6 5 4 3 2

5 6 7 8 9 10

10 9 8 7 6 5

Page 20 • Number Squares (Numbers to 10)

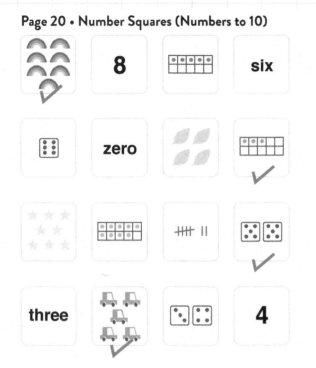

Page 22 • On the Farm

Page 23 • Balloons

Page 24 • Wide Awake

Page 25 • Bouncy Balls

Page 26 • Puzzle Pieces

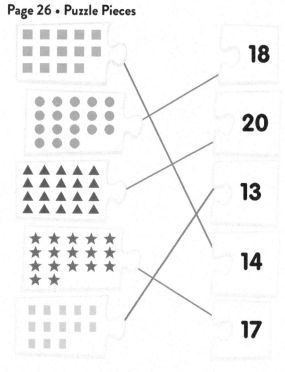

Page 27 • Which Cheetah?

Page 28 • Jack and the Beanstalk

How many magic beans are in my bag?

12

Page 29 • Spider Maze

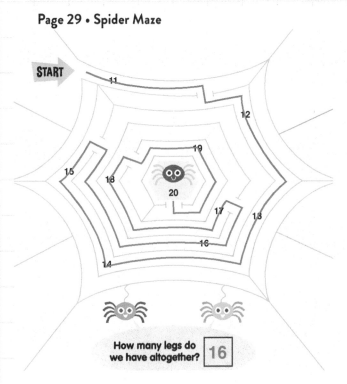

How many legs do we have altogether? 16

Page 30 • Cupcakes

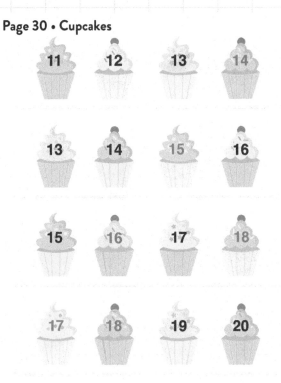

Page 31 • At the Fairground

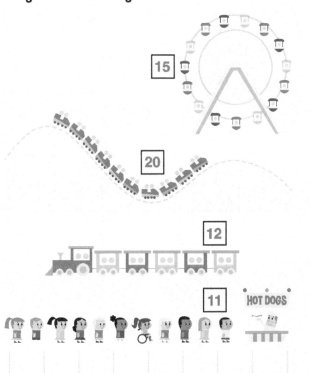

Page 32 • Rainbow Snail

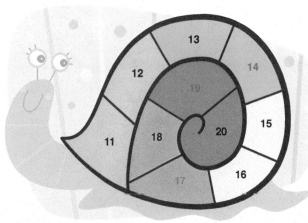

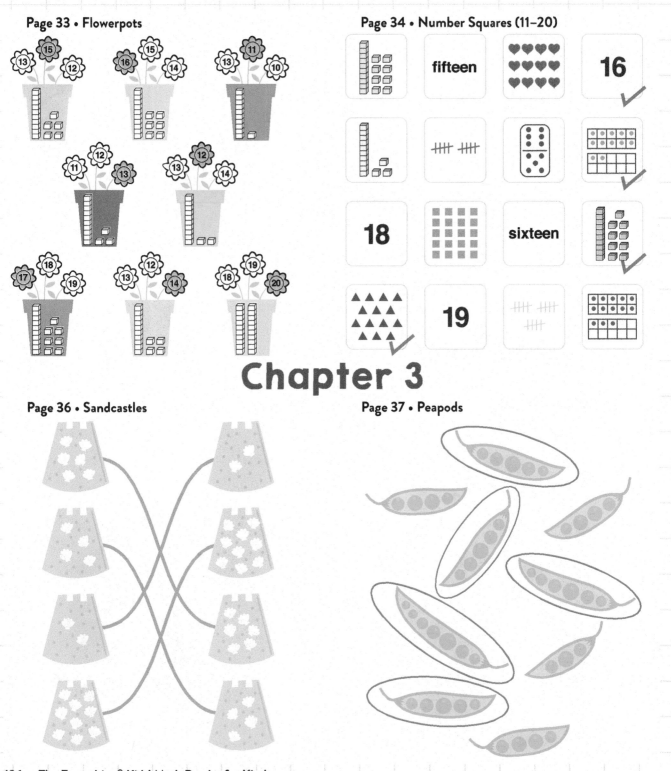

Page 33 • Flowerpots

Page 34 • Number Squares (11–20)

Chapter 3

Page 36 • Sandcastles

Page 37 • Peapods

Page 38 • Butterflies

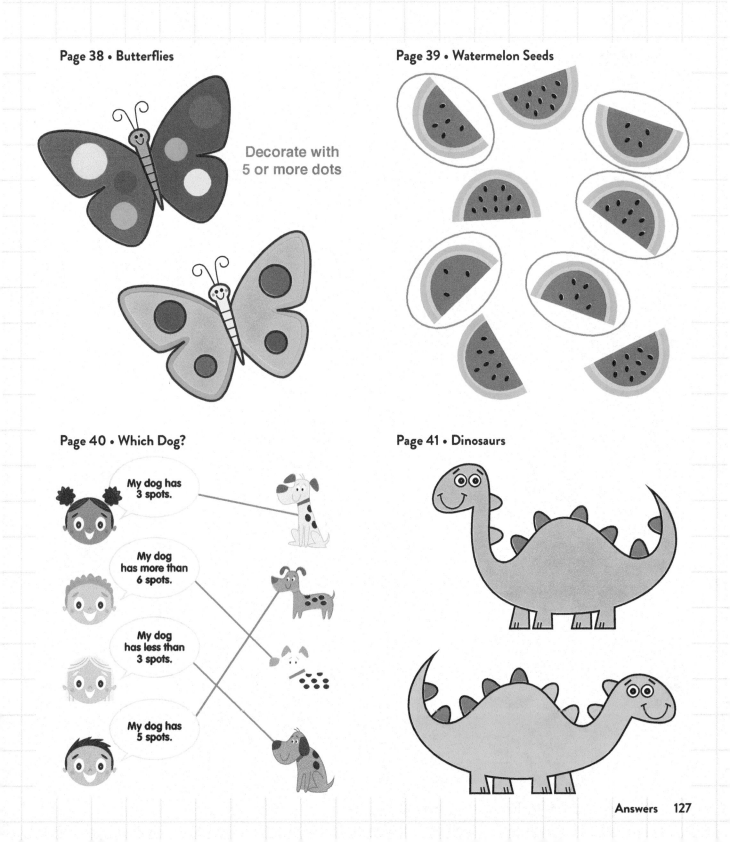

Decorate with 5 or more dots

Page 39 • Watermelon Seeds

Page 40 • Which Dog?

My dog has 3 spots.

My dog has more than 6 spots.

My dog has less than 3 spots.

My dog has 5 spots.

Page 41 • Dinosaurs

Page 42 • Number Pies

Pie 1: 4 3 7 1 → **1**

Pie 2: 6 2 7 0 → **0**

Pie 3: 10 8 9 7 → **7**

Pie 4: 6 9 5 8 → **5**

Page 43 • Crocodiles

3 < 4   9 > 8

10 > 7   1 > 0

2 < 5   3 < 6

8 > 6

Page 44 • Pizzas

>

>

=

<

Page 45 • Marbles

Jar A   Jar B

A B
A B
A B
A B

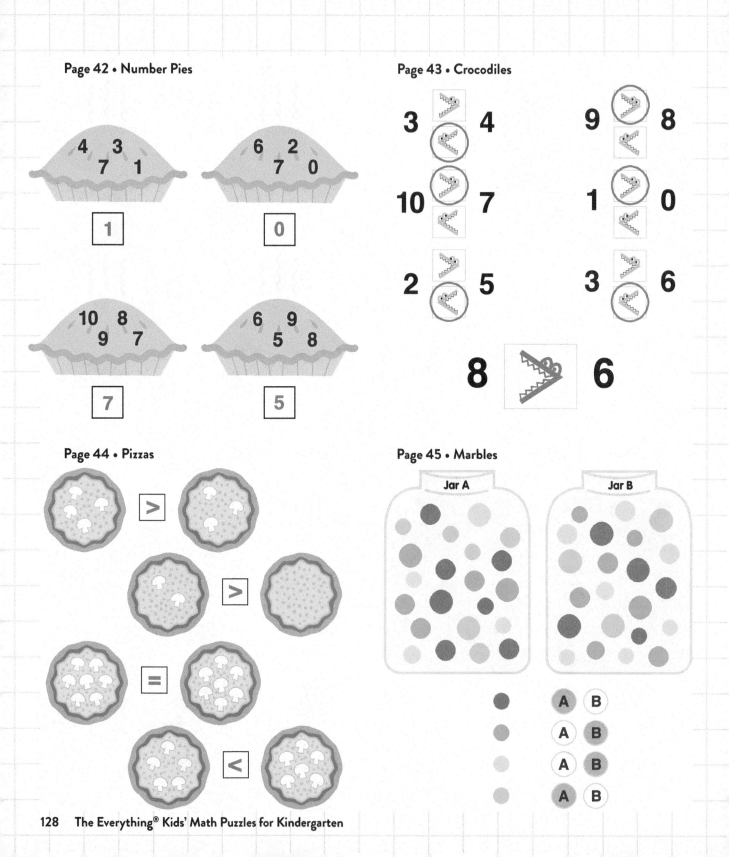

Page 46 • Storming the Castle

Page 47 • Apples

6 > 4
4 = 4
4 < 3
10 < 7
9 > 8
2 = 3
0 < 3
8 > 5

Chapter 4

Page 50 • Houses

20 21 22 23 24 25 26 27 28 29 30

23   29   25

20   30

Page 51 • Polly

Page 52 • Trains

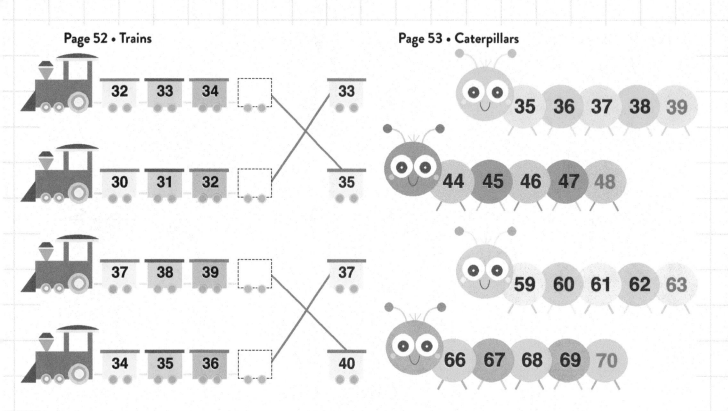

| 32 | 33 | 34 | | 33 |

| 30 | 31 | 32 | | 35 |

| 37 | 38 | 39 | | 37 |

| 34 | 35 | 36 | | 40 |

Page 53 • Caterpillars

35 36 37 38 39

44 45 46 47 48

59 60 61 62 63

66 67 68 69 70

Page 54 • Bird's Nest

40	41	45	53	52
50	42	49	50	51
59	43	44	45	46
51	50	49	48	47
52	53	54	44	58
48	49	55	56	59
60	59	58	57	60

Page 55 • What's My Name?

1	2	3	4	5	6	7	8	9	10
11	12	13	14	15	16	17	18	19	20
21	22	23	24	25	26	27	28	29	30
31	32	33	34	35	36	37	38	39	40
41	42	43	44	45	46	47	48	49	50
51	52	53	54	55	56	57	58	59	60
61	62	63	64	65	66	67	68	69	70
71	72	73	74	75	76	77	78	79	80
81	82	83	84	85	86	87	88	89	90
91	92	93	94	95	96	97	98	99	100

My name is
Jess

Page 56 • Up in the Sky

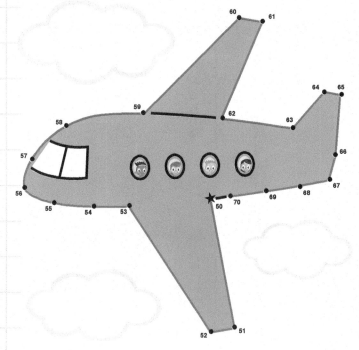

Page 57 • Paint Splatters

1	2	3	4	5	6	7	8	9	10
11	12	13	14	15	16	17	18	19	20
21	22	23	24	25	26	27	28	29	30
31	32	33	34	35	36	37	38	39	40
41	42	43	44	45	46	47	48	49	50
51	52	53	54	55	56	57	58	59	60
61	62	63	64	65	66	67	68	69	70
71	72	73	74	75	76	77	78	79	80
81	82	83	84	85	86	87	88	89	90
91	92	93	94	95	96	97	98	99	100

Page 58 • Who's Swimming?

Page 59 • Counting Crayons

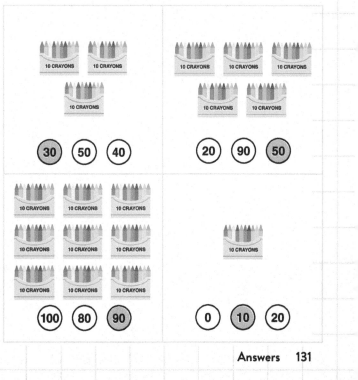

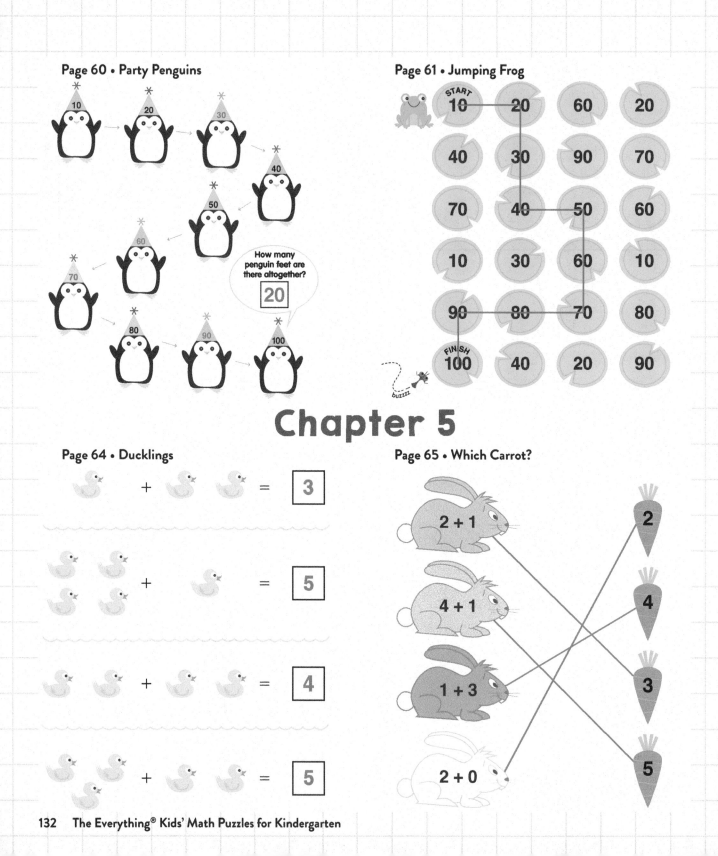

Page 60 • Party Penguins

10 → 20 → 30 → 40 → 50 → 60 → 70 → 80 → 90 → 100

How many penguin feet are there altogether?

20

Page 61 • Jumping Frog

START 10	20	60	20
40	30	90	70
70	40	50	60
10	30	60	10
90	80	70	80
FINISH 100	40	20	90

Chapter 5

Page 64 • Ducklings

🦆 + 🦆🦆 = 3

🦆🦆🦆🦆 + 🦆 = 5

🦆🦆 + 🦆🦆 = 4

🦆🦆🦆 + 🦆🦆 = 5

Page 65 • Which Carrot?

2 + 1
4 + 1
1 + 3
2 + 0

2
4
3
5

Page 66 • Sunflower

Page 67 • Let's Play!

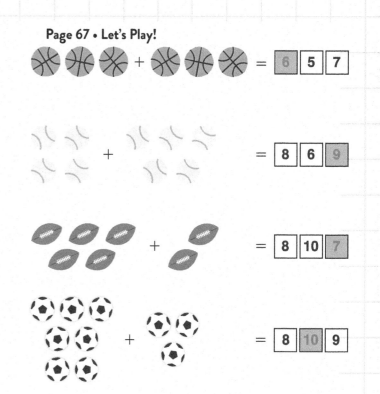

Page 68 • Library Books

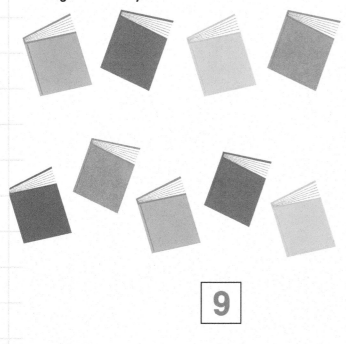

9

Page 69 • In the Rainforest

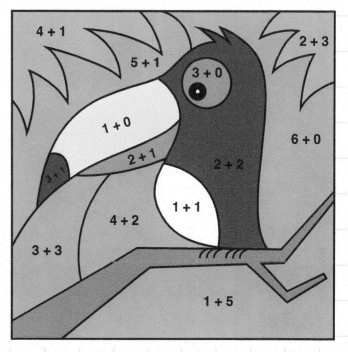

Page 70 • Dice

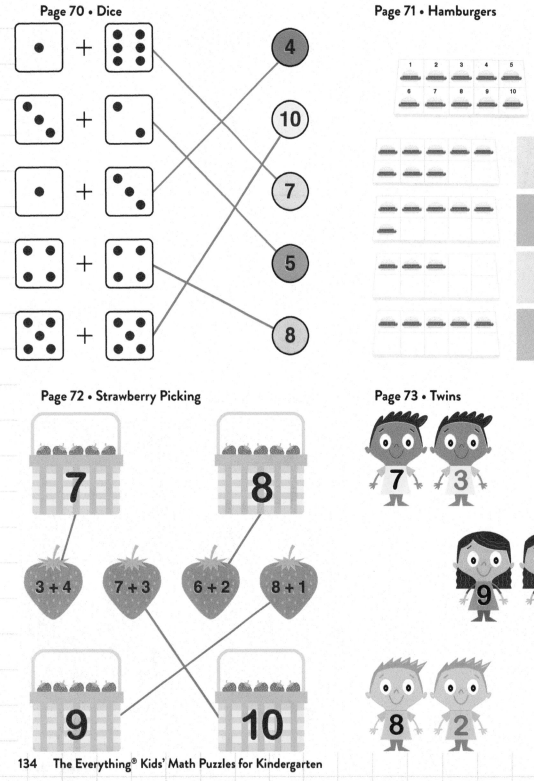

Page 71 • Hamburgers

There are	8		
There are	2	missing	

There are	6		
There are	4	missing	

There are	3		
There are	7	missing	

There are	5		
There are	5	missing	

Page 72 • Strawberry Picking

7   8

3 + 4   7 + 3   6 + 2   8 + 1

9   10

Page 73 • Twins

7   3   5   5

9   1

8   2   6   4

Chapter 6

Page 74 • Hot-Air Balloons

Page 76 • Fruit Salad

$4 - 1 =$ 3

$3 - 3 =$ 0

$5 - 4 =$ 1

$4 - 0 =$ 4

Page 77 • At the Bakery

Page 78 • Hats

Page 79 • Squirrels

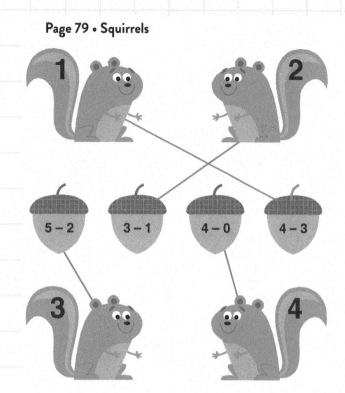

Page 80 • Bears and Honey

I ate 5 jars. How many are left? **5**

I ate 9 jars. How many are left? **1**

I ate 4 jars. How many are left? **6**

I ate 6 jars. How many are left? **4**

Page 81 • Bees

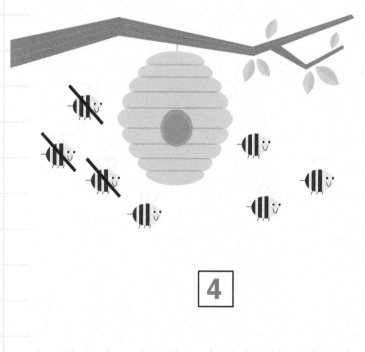

4

Page 82 • Fishing

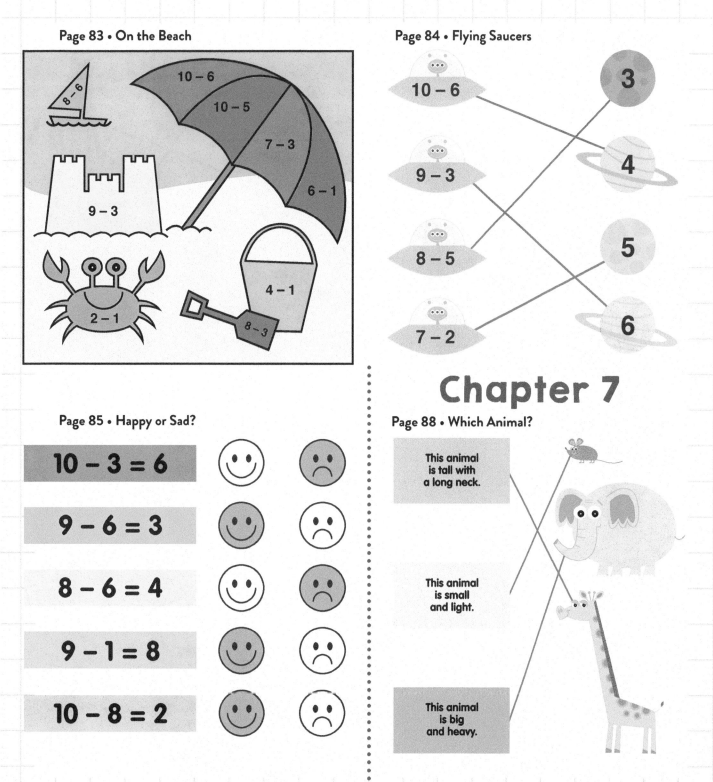

Page 83 • On the Beach

Page 84 • Flying Saucers

Chapter 7

Page 85 • Happy or Sad?

10 − 3 = 6

9 − 6 = 3

8 − 6 = 4

9 − 1 = 8

10 − 8 = 2

Page 88 • Which Animal?

This animal is tall with a long neck.

This animal is small and light.

This animal is big and heavy.

Page 89 • Sorting Socks

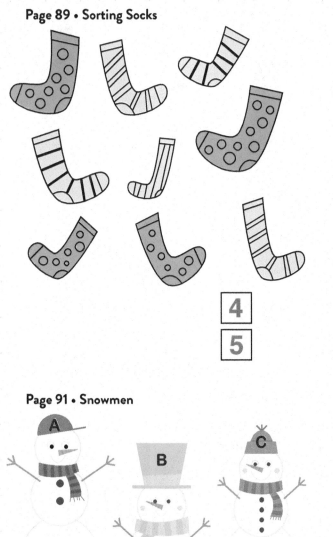

4
5

Page 90 • Legs

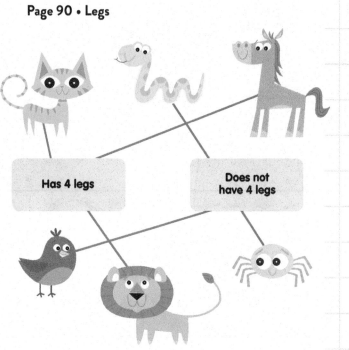

Page 91 • Snowmen

A   B

A   B

C   B

Page 92 • In the Backyard

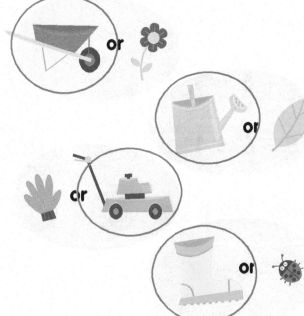

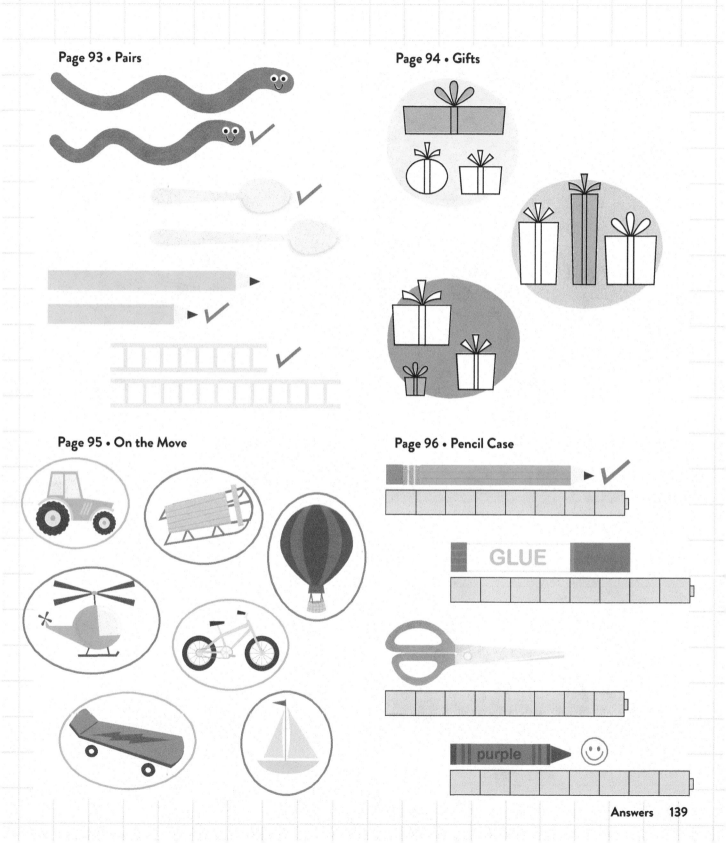

Page 93 • Pairs

Page 94 • Gifts

Page 95 • On the Move

Page 96 • Pencil Case

Page 97 • Enchanted Forest

Page 98 • Water

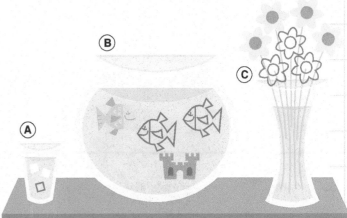

B

A

Page 99 • How's the Weather?

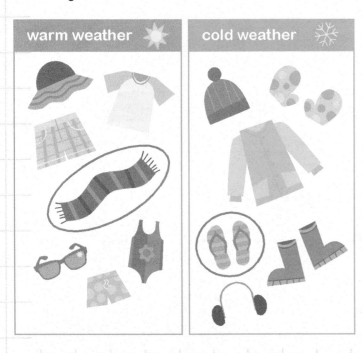

Page 100 • Jelly Beans

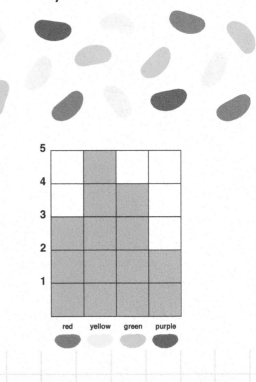

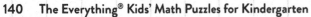

Chapter 8

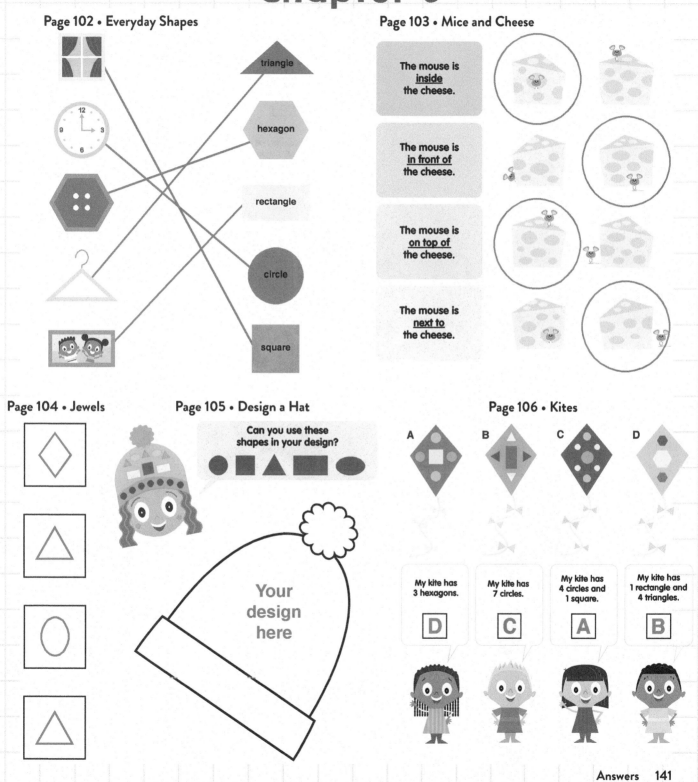

Page 102 • Everyday Shapes

triangle

hexagon

rectangle

circle

square

Page 103 • Mice and Cheese

The mouse is **inside** the cheese.

The mouse is **in front of** the cheese.

The mouse is **on top of** the cheese.

The mouse is **next to** the cheese.

Page 104 • Jewels

Page 105 • Design a Hat

Can you use these shapes in your design?

Your design here

Page 106 • Kites

A B C D

My kite has 3 hexagons.
D

My kite has 7 circles.
C

My kite has 4 circles and 1 square.
A

My kite has 1 rectangle and 4 triangles.
B

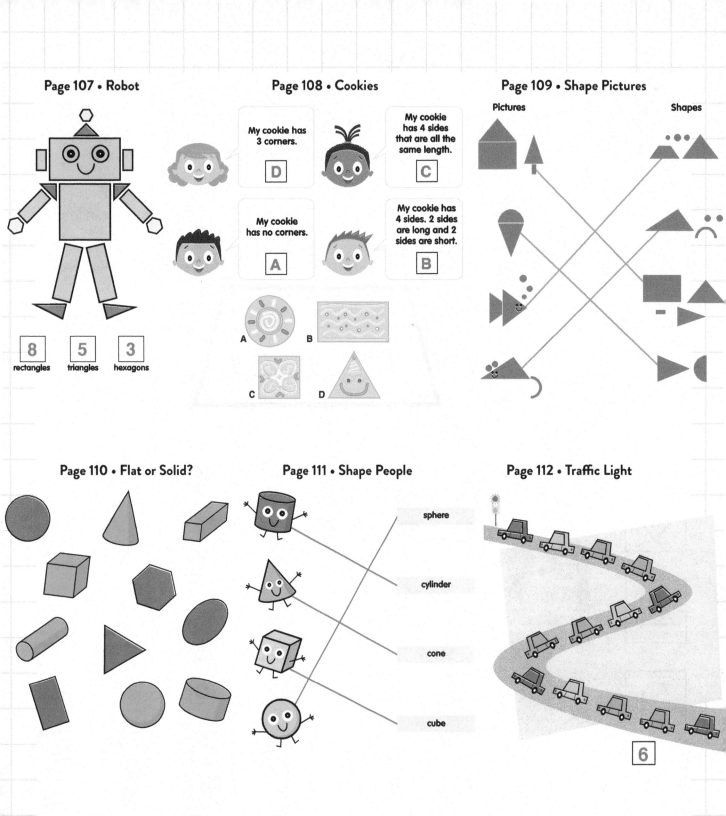

Page 107 • Robot

8 rectangles 5 triangles 3 hexagons

Page 108 • Cookies

My cookie has 3 corners.
D

My cookie has 4 sides that are all the same length.
C

My cookie has no corners.
A

My cookie has 4 sides. 2 sides are long and 2 sides are short.
B

Page 109 • Shape Pictures

Pictures   Shapes

Page 110 • Flat or Solid?

Page 111 • Shape People

sphere

cylinder

cone

cube

Page 112 • Traffic Light

6

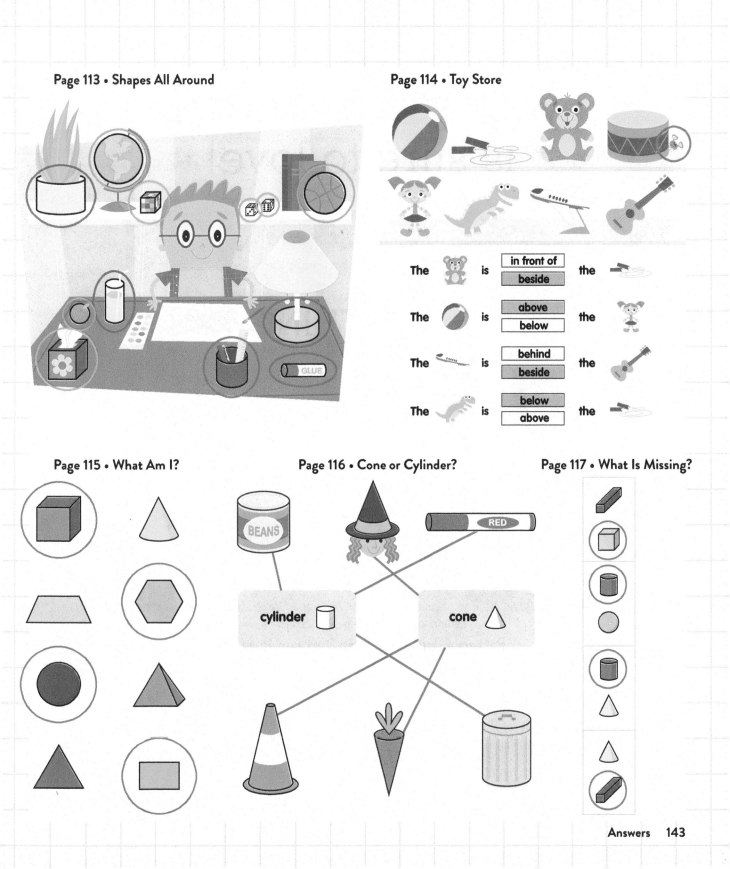

Page 113 • Shapes All Around

Page 114 • Toy Store

Page 115 • What Am I?

Page 116 • Cone or Cylinder?

Page 117 • What Is Missing?